MAPPERTON

Tim Connor

Mapperton, 2021

Dr. Tim Connor was head of history at a major public school and is also an architectural historian. Since retirement to West Dorset he has written, besides academic articles, some detailed accounts of small areas in his immediate neighbourhood. His publication of *Wytherston* (2010) was followed by *North Eggardon Farm* (2015), *West Milton* (2016) and *The Literary and Scientific Institute, Bridport* (2018). What distinguishes *Mapperton* (2021) from these is not only the presence of a well-known house, but also the quality of the documentation for some periods of the life of that small community.

Published by Mapperton Estate
Estate Office, Mapperton, Beaminster DT8 3NR
office@mapperton.com www.mapperton.com

ISBN 978-1-911072-59-1

Originated, printed and bound by Creeds Design & Print Ltd., Bridport, Dorset DT6 3UX

PREFACE

Mapperton is one of those many little places on the English landscape that look like each another until you start examining them closely. In one way it's just a typical small village, a strip of farmsteads surrounding the manor and church. In another, it describes centuries of politics, religion, society and local conflict in one community.

So this book is a history, not a guide, and a work of considerable research. We are all very lucky that the distinguished local historian, Tim Connor, chose to delve into Mapperton's past and unearth the stories of the Morgans, Brodrepps but also many others who lived in this small community. Our family, the Montagus, having inherited a neighbouring estate at Hooke 100 years earlier, only came to Mapperton in 1956.

Anyone who knows the West Country, its hazardous agriculture, its tormented social history and its many stories of in-fighting, lost fortunes and constant change will enjoy this book and recognise its value.

Caroline, John, Julie and Luke Montagu

INTRODUCTION

This is an account of one Dorset parish of about 800 acres over the last five hundred years.

The country between Beaminster and Bridport is difficult to enter or to know. Hidden behind high hedges the motorist sees little. Its low flat-topped hills with their precipitous sides remain accessible only to walkers, most of them sheep. It was not discovered by eighteenth century travellers or by nineteenth century water-colourists; only in the twentieth century has growing publicity brought it to widespread public knowledge. A single rare visitor to Mapperton in the 1770s was entranced by what he called 'one of the most beautiful landscapes ever seen' but that landscape takes some finding now. Nothing much happened there; its buildings have outlasted the families whose countryside this briefly was and no family papers survive with which to humanise them. Tucked in by its own valley, Mapperton epitomises this uncontrived remoteness, just as this history of its inhabitants as far as it can be recovered shows, with occasional shafts of exceptional brightness, how little we know. Before about 1550 just a string of names linked to the place stretch back to Aelmer who the Domesday Book records had held the estate before the Norman Conquest. Romano British farming in the area is to be expected; fragments of roof tiles found below Marsh Farm suggest it and, among the reeds still in a field near there an axe head has been found from the Bronze Age.

In 1774 John Hutchins' *History and Antiquities of the County of Dorset* was published and Richard Brodrepp IV subscribed for four copies. Hutchins's own knowledge of the place, particularly of such details as paintings hanging in the hall, would have been based on visits some years before his own death in 1773. The sequence of families who had owned it and mostly lived there since the thirteenth century ended with Brodrepp's own death in 1774 and thereafter his successors let it to a succession of tenants. Hutchins' account therefore catches the big house at a moment of dissolution. Its contents and perhaps particularly its families' records were ill-cared for, and have disappeared.

This is a 'lockdown' book. Conceived in November 2020 and written in the months that followed, it benefited from a huge amount of information available online, just as it is impoverished by the inaccessibility of archives and libraries where precise enquiry can be sidestepped in favour of the slow, unforeseeable benefits of serendipity. Many of my references to newspaper advertisements have come through the Burney Newspapers or the

Gale Eighteenth Century Online Collection, while salient details of christenings, marriages and burials in parish registers are due to Ancestry. The account begins when it does because the sixteenth century public records begin to allow some knowledge of the people who lived here. But this is not a uniformly documented place; the village is vividly illuminated for a few early modern decades; the house is usually in shadow. Its story had to be, as far as was possible, reconstructed from stray references.

Tim Connor, Powerstock, 2021

Acknowledgements

I am most grateful for unstinting help from John and Caroline Montagu, but many others have helped in different ways, in particular Suky Best; George Brown; Dave Bunney; Jill Channer; John Davies; Chris Fox; Mike Hill; Eleanor Hoare; Michael Hodges; Di Hooley; Liz Jones; Raymond Leaf; Jenny Makepeace; James Miller; Roger Mitchell; Nick Poole, Tim Poole, David Puzey; Francesca Tate; George Tatham; Anna Ware; Thomas Woodcock; the Staff at the Dorset Hist Centre, the Hampshire Archives and Ian Hicks of the Wiltshire and Swindon Archives.

CONTENTS

Short Bibliography

Index

I

Mapperton in the later Sixteenth Century

Tudor Mapperton was a community of something over a hundred people, clustered at three main but quite separate sites within the parish. Some houses would have stood around the medieval church though these have now disappeared. Perhaps the largest group stood on the hill to the northeast around the farm of Coltleigh. A third group lay in the valley to the south west, at a now-vanished hamlet called Mythe with its mill on the stream running south towards Loscombe and on to the sea at Bridport. Isolated at the extreme west one farmstead, later Mapperton Farm, looked over towards Netherbury. This account begins in the mid sixteenth century because it then becomes possible to know details of the lives of at least some inhabitants of these settlements, and to see the houses they built.

In some of these early records one name is conspicuous by its absence, that of Morgan, lords of the manor. The Morgan family had held Mapperton since the fourteenth century when the heiress of the previous lords, Mawd or Mary Bryt had married John Morgan of Morgan Hayes near Sidmouth, Devon, and Mapperton was just one of their several scattered manors. In the early sixteenth century John Morgan is to be found on his estate at Little Comberton, Worcestershire, where he was assessed for the Subsidy on lands worth £40, and was awarded a grant of arms in 1525. Morgan owned other lands in Worcestershire and also in Warwickshire where he died in 1535. It was his son Robert who moved back to Dorset. Perhaps this was connected to his marriage to Mary Wogan, a girl from White Lackington, just over the Somerset border, but the earliest evidence of his being at Mapperton begins in 1545 when he was assessed on lands here worth £26, substantially less than his Worcestershire holdings. His Dorset estate included half the Manor of Wytherston next door to Mapperton, but also lands in Netherbury, Broadwindsor, Allington and Uploders. In 1545 he was in his mid-thirties. By the time he died in 1567 he had three adult sons and four daughters under twenty-one.

What sort of a house Robert and Mary Morgan found when they arrived at Mapperton is unknown. The Bryts would have had a substantial dwelling and barns. No doubt it stood close to the church. Perhaps, after years as the residence of tenants, it was in poor repair. The Morgans now built a new house and proudly proclaimed as much.

Robert Morgan, and Mary his wife, built this house,

in their own life time, at their own charge and cost.

What they spent, that they lent;

What they gave, that they have;

What they left, that they lost.

This was recorded in 1774 as inscribed in the Hall. Though it is now invisible there, it is perhaps Mapperton's most repeated detail. Perhaps it survives behind the great chimneypiece in the hall not installed till 1909. Such inscriptions were not uncommon in sixteenth century houses though few have survived. The final three lines repeat an older adage recorded at locations as widespread as Tiverton, Devon, and St. Albans, both on tombs. Sadly, the Morgans didn't think to add a date.

What survives of this new house is principally the north wing. Its spiral pinnacles above projecting, faceted angle pilasters bear close comparison to an important group of Dorset houses, built in the decades around 1550. Two of the most important are the great house at Melbury Sampford built by1542 and the parlour range at Athelhampton now dated to 1545-9. Further away, the remains of Sir John Horsey's house at Clifton Maybank (1545-50, now

Mapperton, North Wing.

partly re-erected at Montacute) and the finely executed gable-end off the hall at Bingham's Melcombe are comparable. On a smaller scale, the house erected by John Samways after he bought the manor at Toller Fratrum in 1539 also shows some similar features. Because of the use of Ham Hill stone on several of these houses, it has been suggested that these houses were

Athelhampton Hall, North Wing, 1545-9.

the work of a team of masons based at the quarries on Ham Hill, Somerset, and some of these characteristic details may be seen on the exterior of Barrington Court (1550s) in that county. Athelhampton, where Ham stone is employed only for window frames, string courses and decorative enrichments is, albeit rather grander, the closest parallel to Mapperton, while the latter preserves more original detail.

Mapperton, Heraldic beasts on finials of North Wing.

The spiral pinnacles are surmounted by heraldic beasts holding shields of arms. Three of the four on the gable ends at Mapperton appear to retain the original arms of Morgan, Muckleston and Bryt that are also displayed in the panel of contemporary stained glass now in the church. Prominent on the west gable, the Morgan griffin contrasts with the Muckleston

Montacute House. West front, Horsey arms from Clifton Maybank.

dragon. Of the other houses in this group, only the fragment of Clifton Maybank now at Montacute can offer a similar stone heraldic display, albeit considerably reworked in the 1780s. Robert Morgan's house seems to have been unusually rich in heraldic display 'carved on wood or stone, or painted in glass in the windows', some of which was recorded in *c*.1600, although by 1774 Hutchins said much of it was 'now removed or painted over'. These stone finials are a remarkable survival. They announced the arrival of the family in the county, though whether local viewers were able to assess the reputation or even identity of the Staffordshire Mucklestons whose heiress had married into the Bryts nine generations earlier or even the Bryts themselves of eight generations before, may be doubted.

Most intriguing of all, the house at Mapperton is said to have had a two storey 'oriel' window, projecting from the east end of the north wing comparable, perhaps, to the oriel remaining on the west side at Melbury, and of which fragments were visible in 1899. It may have been taken down before 1828 for neither John Buckler and Edward Blore who drew Mapperton at that time seem to have caught sight of this salient feature. What is remarkable is that this showpiece window was not on the entrance front, but overlooking the steep valley to the east.

Mapperton, North West bedroom overmantel.

Besides these significant exterior details, Mapperton also boasts important internal decoration from the mid-sixteenth century. Two overmantels upstairs in the north wing preserve plaster decoration of an early renaissance type. One displays repeated profile heads of a woman and of a warrior that seems to be a version of the pattern used on choir stalls at St Cross, Winchester, erected before 1520. This overmantel carries in the centre the Bryt arms with, at each end, the Morgan crest of griffin's head with 'in its mouth a corn-flag of three leaves', while below it, in the spandrels of the fireplace arch the Morgan griffin and the Bryt lion face each other. The profile heads recur as a frieze in the main

Mapperton, detail of overmantel, warrior head.

Mapperton, principal bedroom: detail of frieze.

Mapperton, principal bedroom, c.1956.

bedroom, beneath a fine plaster ceiling, with pendentives, close to other examples of the work of Somerset plasterers. The ceiling may date from a few decades later than the overmantels, suggesting that Robert and Mary Morgan's house was completed by the next generation, either by their eldest son, the nefarious John, executed for murder of his brother-in-law in 1580, or by his brother Christopher who died in 1591.

Robert Morgan's will of 1567 carefully divided up his properties among his sons and ensured that his brother Edward could continue with his lease of Wytherston. The estate at Wantsley between Beaminster and Broadwindsor went to Christopher, and George got the

Worcestershire lands. His widow Mary was to continue at Mapperton, while the main Dorset estate including lands in Netherbury, Allington and Uploders was charged with raising £400 to be divided among his four young daughters, provided that all of them would obey their mother in the matter of whom they were to marry.

Overshadowing every clause of this confused will was the repeated provision that his heir John was not to interfere with any part of it. He worried lest 'my said sonne John or any other person . . who shalbe my heire do trouble or Disquiet my sonne George' or he feared that John might 'Molest or disquiet my said wyfe of her quiet possession' of what he left to her, and he even tried to insist that if John refused to accept the terms of the will then he should receive no legacy at all. The father clearly bent over backwards to avoid difficulties with his eldest son. John Morgan inherited Mapperton however and lived there between 1567 and the 'incident' in the winter of 1580, invisible to most records. He was nominated a trustee of the extensive estates of his Wogan grandmother when she died in 1574, but those Somerset estates were intended for another grandson, still a minor. Such business would perhaps have continued contact with his mother, now married to the recusant Catholic William Stourton and living at Worminster outside Wells, and with George Speke of White Lackington, where his mother came from.

John Morgan acquired startling prominence when he murdered his brother-in-law Nicholas Turberville at Wells, in January 1580. As Rachel Lloyd told it in her vivid book, *Dorset Elizabethans*, a heated religious argument broke out in which Morgan accused his sister Anne, Turberville's wife, of not sticking to the Catholicism in which she had been brought up. Nicholas Turberville, recently Sheriff of Dorset and necessarily more outwardly conformist, appears to have accused Morgan of expecting too much of his sister while doing little to show his own loyalty to the old faith. Tempers raged and Morgan stabbed Turberville, who died on the spot. Anne Turberville, pregnant with her fifth child, took an active role in bringing her brother to justice and he was hanged at Chard on 14 March, 1580.

The murder became widely known. Two sources survive to show diametrically different aspects of this family tragedy. Within a week a pair of ballads were registered in London, entitled 'A ditty of Master Turberville murdered: and John Morgan that murdered him'. The ballads, heavy handed pieces of high-end doggerel are only known because they were preserved in the manuscript book of a Weymouth merchant, which survived long enough for the texts to have been printed in the 1930s. They work as a pair. The first praises Turberville to the skies; he is the match for or greater than the Homeric heroes and a man of great virtue and moderation in his dealings as a magistrate.

This justlye he a justice lived

to all an upright judge

ffor desarts of all men embraste

in hart he bare no grudge.

The second part of the first ballad opens the tap of invective onto Morgan including the charge that he 'a papist rang'd from Rome'.

The second ballad reverses all this. Morgan is praised, to Turberville's disgrace. And Morgan was much missed. At his execution:

in dolful wyse would dorset then

wth weepinge speend theare dayes

and Somerset be sheed her showers

would linger no delayes.

W^{ch} well appeared at his death

by sighs of ruthfull cryes

that gentlemen of bothe the shires

dyd make wth weepinge eyes.

Further damage to Morgan's reputation occurred in a third account given by the young writer and playwright Anthony Munday in a book published later in 1580. Munday was publishing what purported to be virulently anti-Catholic tracts at that time and this one was a review of several recent murders and suicides taken as 'signs of God's anger towards us [Protestants]'. He describes Morgan 'by common report' to be a 'lewd and wicked liver, and given to swearing, roysting, and all wickednes abounding in him.'

In sharp contrast to this vilification are two letters written by Morgan himself from the gaol in Chard, though here too the originals have disappeared. One, addressed to his mother Mary, shows a resigned self-awareness:

'your son dieth not, but sleepeth till the Lord Jesus Christ revive him, and such life shall not last long. I go to sleep before you but we shall wake together, and after such waking then shall we sleep no more'... 'I used my time so ill that now my time is gone. Whoso abuseth his time shall have his time shut off. Warn you my bretheren this, I pray, and bless them all.'

To his sister Ann, the situation is more complex. He begins 'Even he whom thou hast holpen forth to death, salutes thee':

Take counsel of him which loveth thee no more with natural love; for thou hath quenched it, but with Christian love which thou canst not quench. First, serve God thyself and bring up thy children in His fear...

Their father, I think, would not have died for thee; woe to those babes if you are gone. Trust not these friends of thy husband's side; at last they may have chance to hate thee for me. Thou hast the best natured mother alive. I have written that she may love thee, yet thou art a simple woman in an open field…

He is not in case now to lie that write thee these, therefore believe him… Forgive me and pray for me. Written by the dying hand of sometimes thy brother, now by thee overthrown'.

It is impossible to give an adequate context for these remarkable texts and for a sequel there is only silence. Morgan recognises his own wretched position with regard to his sister but, understanding her vulnerability, 'a simple woman in an open field', seeks the best for her and her family. When his mother Mary Stourton came to make her own will in 1595 only two of her daughter Ann's children, Troilus and Cassandra, appear to have survived. That she calls them her children rather than the grandchildren they were may indicate that she had had to bring them up.

Uncertainty in a Catholic family about how far to conform to the Elizabethan regime is wholly unsurprising at this time. Their argument flared at a particularly anxious moment in the relationship between the English Catholics and the government. In 1570, after a decade of relative calm, the Pope had excommunicated Queen Elizabeth so that for some Catholics at least, full allegiance to the sovereign was impossible, and the imprisoned figure of Mary Queen of Scots presented a glamorous alternative. In Dorset the Protestant reformation had as yet made little impact. Religious administration of the county was divided between two authorities, the new, impoverished and often vacant see of Bristol and the Dean of Salisbury who was responsible for thirty of its parishes including Mapperton. In these circumstances the conservative example of the major local Catholic families, the Arundells at Chideock or the Paulets at Hooke was powerful, and it is not surprising that the Morgans should behave likewise. The ballad touched on Catholics' varying degrees of conformity to the Elizabethan regime in an unusually vivid way:

Why shouldest thou muster morgan nowe
the papist rankes Among?
What need the woodcock blame the snight [snipe]
for that his beake is longe?

[Two birds with outstandingly long bills should not be arguing which is longest.]

All this coincided with beginnings of the a resolute effort at conversion, epitomised by the arrival of young Jesuit priests trained abroad intent on recovering England for the Catholic church, of whom the most famous was Edmond Campion S.J., hung, drawn and quartered at

Tyburn on 1 December 1581.

This new zeal also epitomises John Munden of Coltleigh in Mapperton, one of the most exceptional figures in the history of this parish. The eldest son of John Munden (d.1574) the tenant of Coltleigh, he was a scholar at Winchester College in 1555 then at New College, Oxford where he had begun as probationary Fellow only to be deprived of that comfortable living for refusing to take communion in 1566. Thereafter he returned as a rural schoolmaster at Netherbury and perhaps also at Dorchester, till in October 1580 he went abroad to the Catholic college at Rheims. Travel abroad without licence was forbidden at this time precisely to prevent such religious emigration; Munden lost all he had and arrived at the seminary destitute. In the following summer he went to Rome where he was ordained priest and stayed for some months. Returning to England in 1582 he was almost immediately arrested at Hounslow perhaps on his way west, and was sent to the Tower of London. With three companions he was executed in 1584.

It is an extraordinary coincidence that, of the vanishingly few writings to survive of anyone who lived at Mapperton before the twentieth century, two should date from the sixteenth century, should have been written within a few years of each other, and both should be final letters of men about to be executed. For John Morgan's (lost) letter from Chard gaol is matched by John Munden's, now preserved at Stonyhurst. It is addressed to 'Cousin Duche', perhaps to a member of the Douch family of Coltleigh and so someone with whom he had grown up:

> 'I am warned to prepare against tomorrow to go to dye, & yet I hope in Jesus Christ to live for ever, & having almost forgotten you and others my friends was like to have passed you in silence...'

The letter turns to send good wishes to other friends: to his old headmaster at Winchester, to Robert Farnham, a slightly older contemporary from school and New College who lived beyond Broadwindsor, and the leaders of the English college at Rheims, 'bidding you faire well for ever in this world'.

George Bowden

A third letter, one of a small group of petitions, provides a complete contrast to the dramatic final epistles of Morgan and Munden, and bring us close to the lived experience in Mapperton itself. These concern the irruption of a new clergyman into the parish, a tactless puritan who threw the world of the conservative inhabitants into angry disarray.

By the mid 1590s the Rector Peter Beauchamp was an old man, having been appointed during the reign of Queen Mary forty years before and having lived through momentous changes in the nature of the church in England. About the time of his appointment in the 1550s he was described as 'gallicus', one of several 'French' priests in the county and, in common with most of the mid-Tudor priesthood in the diocese, as 'no graduate'. While the Morgans remained loyal to the old religion little more than a minimum may have changed in the parish over forty years. This quiet conservative corner was suddenly confronted by the new puritanism when George Bowden, an Oxford graduate who may have been born in Lyme Regis, turned up in the area. He had been licensed initially as a schoolmaster for the diocese of Bristol but he also seems to have elbowed the elderly Beauchamp from his role as priest. His actions met immediate opposition from the little community, expressed with growing fury in a number of 'presentments' delivered to the Dean of Salisbury responsible for the parishes under his jurisdiction.

Presentments were usually responses to set questions concerning the conduct of church services, the material upkeep of church property and also the moral behaviour of the parishioners, presented at an annual visitation of the parish by whoever exercised jurisdiction over it, usually the bishop of the diocese but, in the case of Mapperton, the Dean of Salisbury. So, in the 1560s the churchwardens had presented that the churchyard wall and the 'wyndowes' were 'in decaye'. At another time they admitted that they needed to provide a new surplice for their minister. But in 1597 the churchwardens abandoned normal presentments such as these to have a letter written on their behalf direct to the Dean to express altogether greater anxieties. The surplice turned out to be just the start. One had been provided, and at some expense, but

> 'As we were appointed by our deane of Sarum to provide a fit and decent serplis by christmas day … which surplis was provided …And was offered unto hym tweis before morning prayer And he did refuse yt[.]'

Later correspondence makes it abundantly clear that Bowden's refusal to wear the priestly surplice was a principled stand against what he saw as a relic of popery and a perversion of the true role of the clergy. But refusing to wear the surplice was only a beginning to his novel ideas. Not only was he opposed to standing up to hear the gospel, but

> 'our minester george bowden hathe taken our commnion tabell borde out of our churche and hath put him to An offis in his house and doth hull hys Dishshes uppon.'
> 'moreover we had no servis on michael mas daye and againe on saynt lukes daye and agayne on saynt Adrewes dayes and A lyttell serv(is) on candlemas daye /in the morning/ and after ward he went to bemister and preched.'

More significantly than the failure to observe the old feast days, Bowden held forth on crucial matters of doctrine concerning salvation:

> 'moreover he dothe (sa)ye the best woorkes that we doo ys synne and abhomynation
> and filthines before god[.]
>
> moreover he doth saye that a childe when that he ys borne he [is] apoynted to be
> damned or saved'

Over the next nine months three other letters were written for the illiterate churchwardens, each expressing similar outrage. The most interesting of them widens the issue to suggest a more general political awareness among the inhabitants of Coltleigh, Mythe and Mapperton. Bowden's refusal to wear the surplice, along with his 'bitter Inventions [and] disdaynfull glansinge wordes' meant that:

> he doth very much abuse queenes lawes [.] … he that ys pointed to governe in the
> church and doe teache and instruct well ys worthy of doubbell honor so likewise
> those that neglect theire duty worthy of doubbell punishment for what [preserveth]
> the comen wealthe beste but whan the mynisters and subjects obaye the …
> maiestrates[magistrate's] lawes … but some hath gon so far beyonde the bowndes of
> modestie in serchinge & rippinge the blessinges and infirmities of others that theire
> doinges ys all moste come to an open contempt[.]

These vivid protests got nowhere. When Beauchamp died in April 1599, George Bowden was installed as Rector of Mapperton, a position he occupied till his death forty-one years later.

One explanation for this decisive change of religious leadership lies with the man who exercised the right of patronage, the then lord of the manor. In 1599 this was John Luttrell (1566-1620) briefly an MP for Minehead, who had married Christopher Morgan's widow Ann, lived in the big house and farmed the estate during the minority of his step-daughters, Elizabeth and Ann. Some idea of his religious opinions became apparent during the argument about how the controversial surplice should be paid for. The churchwardens believed that as patron, Luttrell should meet half the cost, which he had refused. Luttrell was not being mean for he offered to pay the whole sum, but

> master luttrell doth find greate fault with us for that we brought one of so grate A prise
> and sayethe we might put our mony to a better use[.]

It appears that Luttrell shared Bowden's contempt for elaborate vestments and other sources showing him supporting Bowden against recusant Catholics within the parish suggest that he sympathised with Bowden's enforcement of reformed Protestant worship.

The change from a conservative response to the religious changes of the period to one that was, with little tact or forbearance, actively promoting them had other significant effects. If one were to ask when Mapperton church was finally purged of its pre Reformation decoration, statues, lights, perhaps wall paintings and stained glass, the most likely answer would be during Bowden's long incumbency. And with those relics of an old world went communal activities such as the traditional 'Beating of the Bounds' or perambulation of the parish boundaries. Bowden's refusal to take part in this had been yet another item on the parishioners' list.

But some accommodation was reached. As the years went on he is to be found witnessing his parishioners' wills and assessing their inventories. He married, had three children, and when he died his possessions were, by the standards of other local clergy of the time, not grand: a silver bowl, a dozen silver spoons and a silver seal worth £5.10s. 9d. Otherwise his possessions did not mark him out from the husbandmen and tenant farmers of his congregation: nine pewter platters, 'two fruit dishes two saults two candlesticks, three chamberpots' and, in the study '4 shelves and the Bookes prized att £5 6s. 8d'.

Bowden's continuing presence in the parish may also have been influential with the next inhabitant of the manor house, the husband of Christopher Morgan's younger heiress Mary, Richard Brodrepp, whose later career shows him to have been an active supporter of radical politics. The older of Morgan's heiress daughters, Elizabeth briefly married a Devon man and then Sir Thomas Trenchard of Wolfeton, while Mary's marriage to Richard Brodrepp followed in about 1607. In 1615 a division of their estate was concluded between the two heiresses, now that both were married and with heirs. In this some local lands like Wytherston were absorbed into the estates of the Trenchards, and Mary retained the house and estate of Mapperton with the Morgan lands in Worcestershire.

Richard Brodrepp's origins are obscure. The surname occurs in the registers of several Somerset parishes in the early seventeenth century, at Wells and around Bruton, and all may originate from the village of Bawdripp east of Bridgewater. His marriage settlement of May 1607 mentions his widowed mother Dorothy as of Hunstile, a farm near Goathurst, south-west of Bridgewater. The Goathurst register of burials includes an unusually precise reference to the burial of Alice, 'ye daughter of Mrs. Dorothy Brodrip widdow of Hunstill who was buried in ye body of ye church' in 1596. The title 'Mistress', and being able to afford burial within the church offer slight claims to social status, and the name of Dorothy was to be preserved in the Mapperton family. There is no record of Richard Brodrepp's baptism, but he would have been at least twenty-one on his equally unrecorded marriage in *c.* 1607.

II

The Brodrepps and Local Politics, 1607-1706

For a hundred years Mapperton was dominated by the lives of two men, Richard
Brodrepp I, who died in 1657, and his grandson, Richard II, who succeeded his father
Christopher two years later, and died in 1706. Neither would avoid involvement in the
divisive, violent and rapidly changing politics of the century, but they appear to have
approached them from a shared standpoint.

Entering the county from outside on his marriage, Richard Brodrepp could not rely on
an established network of family alliances and support; when the heralds made a visitation to
record the genealogies of the county families soon after he arrived, the family at Mapperton
was not examined. In his brother-in-law Sir Thomas Trenchard, Member of Parliament and
Sheriff in 1634 however, Brodrepp had a connection with one of the most established and
powerful families in the area. Trenchard was known as 'a favourer of puritans' and all one
learns of Richard I's activities shows that he shared his brother-in-law's opinions. Through
Trenchard he would have met other powerful politicians in the county such as Denzil
Holles of Dorchester, MP for the county town, son of an earl and an intransigent political
activist. Trenchard would also have provided him with an introduction at second hand
into the business of county government. In his year as sheriff Trenchard was responsible
for the implementation of controversial Ship Money tax, now levied in time of peace. In
this first year, 1634, he raised nearly 80% of the sum demanded, but he also sent in a list of
those refusing to pay that included John Browne of Frampton, Sir Richard Strode and Sir
John Millar of Came, all significant west Dorset gentry who resented what they saw as the
'arbitrary' nature of Charles I's government. Trenchard's local influence was also powerful
in the corporate borough of Bridport, a town then declining somewhat with its harbour silting
up and having suffered a cruel visitation of the plague in 1627. Perhaps the most significant
introduction there would have been to Sir Thomas's brother-in-law, another influential local
puritan, John Browne of Frampton, Ship Money refuser, MP for the borough and later for the
county itself.

It is the support of men like these, more or less united in their religious convictions
and, what was almost indistinguishable from that, in their political opinions, that explains

why in early March 1643 Richard Brodrepp should be one of the first to be appointed to what became the Dorset County Committee. This was one of the institutions that Parliament evolved to replace the traditional forms of county government that, with the beginning of civil war in the previous autumn, were mostly in royalist hands. He may have raised a troop of horse for parliament in the preceding months, his younger son John certainly did, but he was clearly known as a committed man among like-minded men at Westminster. The Committees' responsibilities grew piecemeal. Initially they were charged with the central task of raising money for Parliament's armies by means of a weekly assessment, which turned out to be every bit as heavy and irksome as Ship Money had been only a few years earlier. To this was added a few weeks later the sequestration of estates of 'delinquents' [royalists] in order to help raise those funds, and these twin activities developed as the need for money got more pressing. A Standing Committee was established the following month, with Brodrepp a member. A third important function of Committee was to attend to church affairs. They were in charge of sequestering the estates of 'delinquent' clergy, and administering the incomes of these livings. This caused many small-scale personal tussles throughout the area, of which the continuing conflict with William Gollop, the 'delinquent, scandalous and malignant' Rector of Stoke Abbott, was typical. Refusing outright the edict of the Committee, he was imprisoned at Weymouth and when released continued to farm his glebe as if nothing had happened. Someone had to be sent to Stoke Abbot to try to reach a settlement.

Because of the rare survival of the minute books of the Standing Committee from 1646 to the beginning of 1650, one can watch Brodrepp working with his colleagues, at meetings in Sherborne, Blandford, Dorchester and once having to accompany a troop of horse from Wareham to Shaftesbury, dealing with matters small and large: 40s for a 'maymed souldier' wounded at the siege of Corfe, or deciding who should manage the utterly various pieces of property arising from the estates of sequestered royalists. A typical case was very close to home. Brodrepp's land bordered the sprawling Hooke estate of the devout Catholic and scholarly royalist John Paulet, Marquess of Winchester, whose woodland crested the hill opposite Coltleigh. His main house at Basing in Hampshire had been besieged, wrecked and demolished by parliamentary forces just a few months earlier. Now in the autumn of 1646 Hooke was burnt by parliamentary soldiers and Henry Samways of North Poorton and a loyal supporter of the new regime to which he'd contributed £8 was claiming he had been living in the house at Hooke and suffered £60 of damage. Management of Hooke's valuable woodland was a more important matter; the Committee carefully assessed competing versions of what had happened to the income before deciding that Paul Minterne, probably a relative of the Paulets' agent Hugh, was attempting to profiteer on his own account. He was pronounced 'malignant and ill affected to Parliament' and 'an unfitt man to be imployed in the service of the State'. Matters dragged on for a year then perhaps due to the influence of a fellow Committeeman Walter Foy of Bubb Down, and a kinsman of the Minternes, Paul was reinstated as collector of all the estate rents, made responsible for covering the house to prevent further ruin, and to stabilise the management of the woodland, for a salary of £8.6s.8d.

In one area this government by tiny details promised a much-needed reform in the attempt to redistribute clerical incomes to supplement poorly endowed parishes from income of small or vanished parishes. It was proposed, for example that the £50 income of the sinecure of Wytherston, where its church was long ruined and its inhabitants already attending Powerstock, should go to supplement that of Powerstock. A list of 43 impoverished parishes was drawn up, including the three Dorchester parishes where the incumbents received an income barely more than a skilled artisan. For whatever reason it was also proposed to increase the income of Mapperton from £60 to £100. Nothing happened; much more recently the Church of England has taken more than century to deal with this problem.

These committeemen, such as Walter Foy or John Whiteway of Dorchester, both of whom Brodrepp met at least forty times in under three years, must have been part of his social life as were his relations by marriage: Browne, Trenchard and William Rose of Wootton Fitzpaine, although they only attended five times together. In the late 1640s Brodrepp must have been in his sixties. I doubt he had ever been so busy.

After the standing Committee's functions were largely taken back to the central administration nothing more is known of Richard Brodrepp until in September 1656 he wrote his will. In an age when wills often employed formulaic phrases whether religious or legal Brodrepp's personal testament reveals his unostentatious piety.

> 'Item I committ my body to be decently not costly entombed by my deare pretious and faithfull wife.
>
> Item my faithfull dutifull and obeydient children whom I love in the Lord soe love you one another then shall you bee as a threefold cord and beloved of God both ioyntly and severally.

Material possessions interest him little. At that time many yeomen or even husbandmen possessed more silver than just twelve spoons.

> Item alle my Stocke of plate beinge one dozen of Silver Spoones I give equally to my Children being now my two Sonnes.
>
> Item I give my Sonne John the bed and cloathes whereon hee lies two paire of Sheetes a sett of red taffery Curtens redd rugg and vallence.

Item I owe nothinge to anie man but love and I have ever willingly paid it to my power.

Item I give to my Sonne Christopher all my other goods and doe make him my Sole executor beinge asoured hee will performe all things proper to mee and mine in love and uprightnes of heart which I beare toward my neighbours …

Item I give to my ever loveing kind and faithful pastor Mr Gundry a gowne

The generosity of intention towards his tenants is unusual:

Item I give to my neighbours Tenants in Coltley and Meeth by name Richard Munden John Birt John Symes John Roper John Mintern Giles Hitt als. Phelps and Giles his sonne to each of them a Cloake intreating them to live in unity and to attend gods ordinances conscionably.

Item I give old Thomas Knight fourty Shillings

Item I give toward placing abroad [as apprentices] the five young Sonnes of Cicely Turner five poundes

Now haveing run my race and come unto the Goal Lord pardon all my Sinns Sweet Christ receive my Soule:

In this true faith I dye By Christ to live eternally Ric: Brodrepp.

Outside the Mapperton community, Brodrepp also gave £10 towards funding a workhouse in Beaminster (the town had been ravaged by fire after the royalist occupation in May 1644), which he had begun and its treasurer was to be another nonconformist minister like, if not as staunch as, his 'loveing kind and faithful pastor' Hugh Gundry.

When he died, sometime in 1657, Brodrepp could not have known that the regime he had served so conscientiously would barely survive him. Royalist risings and the deep unpopularity and great expense of yet another revision at local government under the Major Generals prompted some like Edward Montagu in the Council of State to offer the crown to Oliver Cromwell, only 8 years after the King's execution. But Cromwell would not or could not desert the 'base' he had created in the army, and the matter of the succession was urgent. No solution was found. 'Restoration' of the monarchy proved a fairly painless success in early 1660, at least to start with.

The change in Richard Brodrepp's will from thinking of his children as 'a threefold cord' to making legacies to 'now my two Sonnes' may suggest that another child had very recently died. Whether son or daughter is unknown, but the will of his fellow Committeeman Richard Rose of Wootton Fitzpaine a year later refers to his 'brothers' (a term often used to include brothers-in-law) John and Christopher Brodrepp, and it disposes of the manor of Morgan Hayes, as if that property had passed to the Rose family perhaps through a marriage of one of Richard Brodrepp's daughters. Of Christopher, Richard's heir, little is known, for he died intestate in 1659, only a couple of years after his father. His wife Catherine's will remembered their seven children, such as John to whom she left her gold seal ring, and Christopher £100 'for placing him an Apprentice to a Merchant if he shall soe dispose himself and bee an Apprentice,… otherwise he is not to have the same'. Catherine Brodrepp had been a wealthy woman, leaving estates in trust worth £4700 which Richard II, Christopher's heir was free to liquidate in the interests of his siblings.

Richard Brodrepp II enjoyed the university and Inns of Court education common among his landowning contemporaries; he is thought to have owned 1,000 acres, and his mother's wealth made possible easier circumstances than those of his Cromwellian grandfather. But he too was to live at close quarters to violence and rebellion during the second great crisis of the century. Coming of age following the deaths of his grandfather and father, he may have been spared from local hostility to supporters of the discredited Cromwellian regime. In the winter of 1662-3 he married the daughter of Robert Hunt of Compton Pauncefoot, MP for Ilchester and 'the most reputed justice in Somerset' who had navigated the political difficulties of the Interregnum years with careful discretion. Catherine gave birth to at least seven boys in the ensuing years; several died very young and she died herself a fortnight after the birth of a second John in May 1679. The link with the Hunts remained close, cemented by a further marriage two generations later.

With a growing family it is not surprising that Richard II should turn his attention to his house which had been little altered for almost a century. The only intervention that can be dated

Mapperton, screens passage.

Mapperton, niches in porch.

to the early seventeenth century concerns the woodwork of the screens passage, with its bulging pilasters, similar to that at nearby Melplash, and the paired niches with distinctive inverted scallop tops in the lower storey of the entrance porch. This feature occurs on a number of buildings by or attributed to the architect William Arnold (d. 1637) including Montacute, Lulworth Castle and Cranborne Lodge. A connection, of sorts, with Arnold exists in that the occupant of Mapperton between the early 1590s and at least until the marriage of Mary Morgan with Richard Brodrepp I in 1607 was John Luttrell, whose brother Geoffrey employed Arnold at Dunster Castle in 1617, a commission that ended in a lawsuit.

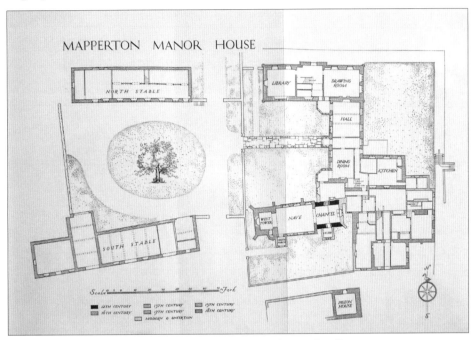

Mapperton, plan. [Historic England]

Richard II now rebuilt the west facing hall range incorporating the kitchens and offices behind. This work appears to have taken place in the mid 1660s: an inscription in the porch has been read as 1661 or 1666. The facade displays seven bays of carefully proportioned, unpedimented cross mullioned windows, of which the outer bays jut forwards to balance the central porch. The care shown in the disposition of these elements may be appreciated by comparison between Sir Roger Pratt's original design for Kingston Lacy (1663) and the squashed application of similar elements at Brympton d'Evercy

Mapperton, entrance front.

Brympton D'Evercy, Somerset, west front.

It is not clear whether the size of the house was much increased for all its fashionable new dress.

In the Hearth Tax levy in the autumn of 1664, probably before building commenced, the house was assessed at ten hearths. This invites comparison with local houses such as George Penne's manor house at Toller Whelme at eight hearths, while Melplash had nine and Parnham eighteen, but the up-to-date character of the new work distinguished it from these local examples.

(*c*.1670). The Kingston Lacy elevation also demonstrates the role of the roof dormers in creating a vertical accent now somewhat reduced at Mapperton by the later addition of a balustrade. Inside, little survives from this period beyond some bolection moulded chimney pieces, such as in the dining room.

Mapperton, dining room chimneypiece.

Toller Whelme, Manor House.

Parnham House, engraving of 1774.

Mapperton, North stable.   *Beaminster Manor, stable.*

Brodrepp also built the dovehouse in 1665, and rebuilt the stables. The south block is dated 1670 and both resemble the stables at the manor house in Beaminster, built for the lawyer John Hoskyns. The windows of both blocks are dressed with elaborate pediments

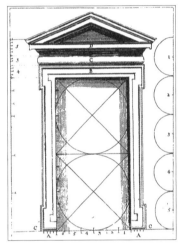

*G. Richards, First Book...
of...Palladio, 1663, pl. 57.*

and eared surrounds suggesting that these subsidiary buildings were the work of a local mason, aware of the new architectural pattern books being published in London. The doorways of both buildings are closely modelled on a plate in *The first book of Architecture of Andrea Palladio,* published in 1663. The disposition of the two stable wings, with the north one continuing the axis of the old 1550 north-west wing of the main house, while the partly older south wing continues the splayed orientation of the chapel, rather than attempting to straighten it into a parallel sided lower court, balances symmetry with pragmatism, the more so because its carriage entrance juts forward thus to provide a degree of closure to the court.

This was a gentleman's house, much more sophisticated than nearby Toller Whelme or the house of the Hillarys at Meerhay, but smaller than Parnham or Chantmarle where the Strodes, Members of Parliament and knighted for three generations, dominated the locality. An indication of the family's social position can be also seen in a succession of younger sons involved in trade, although it is not always possible to place them exactly on a family tree. George Brodrepp, for example, was left £350 by his father John Brodrepp of Yondover in 1690, 'when he is out of apprenticeship'; similarly another George, a younger brother of Richard II, was indeed apprenticed to a London haberdasher and died in 1699. By contrast another brother of Richard II, John Brodrepp of Mapperton described as a 'marchant' on his inventory, died on a visit to Leyden in about 1683. An inventory of his 'Trunck' lists silver items, an inkhorn, a taster, a money box and a silver rapier, as well as some books and a violin which seem more like the indulgences of a pleasure trip than a merchant's stock in trade.

Into the peace of the early Restoration years, and the domestic world of Brodrepp's young family, erupted plague. London had been devastated by this last great outbreak of bubonic plague in 1665, but impact through England in the following months was patchy. About 10% of parishes appear to have been affected. No heightened burial rate is evident in the surviving burial registers of Broadwindsor, Stoke Abbott, or Loders, but at Powerstock burials rose from an average of eighteen in the previous few years to forty-nine in 1668. June 29th saw three burials there in a day. And it is said that the Bell Stone on the western spur of Eggardon marked the furthest point neighbours would go to leave food for the afflicted villagers down in the valley. The impact at Mapperton may have been similar. The village's own burial records for the period are missing, as are those of Netherbury and Beaminster, so it is impossible to form a detailed picture, but the catastrophe had lasting effects on the shape of the settlement. As Hutchins wrote, 'the tenants almost all dying of the plague, 1666, the tenements fell into the lord's hands, and have been all pulled down'. The isolated site of the big house at Mapperton is not the result of some energetic eighteenth-century squire clearing away a hamlet to 'improve' his view, as occurred at Milton Abbas, but the work of plague. Until a few years ago, it was possible to see on a stump of the 'Posy Tree' at the entrance to a track called Dead Man's Lane leading west down towards Netherbury, a plaque saying that during the plague of 1666-7, this marked the furthest that people from Netherbury would allow bodies from Mapperton to be taken on their way to burial. As a result, plague bodies are said to have been buried at South Warren Hill where Hutchins said 'human bones are frequently dug up… in sight of Netherbury church'.

The political world that Richard II tentatively entered in the years after 1670 was rancorous, polarised and unstable, as much locally as nationally. Any hope that the antagonisms of the Civil War and Interregnum might have been buried in an Act of Oblivion at the Restoration had evaporated in a vicious reassertion of cavalier supremacy. Royalists took control of town governments. By expelling ministers like Hugh Gundry who refused to conform to the Prayer Book they took control of the church. As the 1670s progressed also, disquieting signs emerged that Catholicism, now embodied in the military aggression of Louis XIV's France, was again a real threat. But whereas in Queen Elizabeth's reign, that threat had been one of invasion by Spain, now it could seem that the threat was inside the court at Whitehall. In 1672 Charles II took England to war on the side of France and issued a Declaration of Indulgence allowing freedom of worship to Roman Catholics. Yet more disturbing was the matter of the succession. The king had no legitimate heir and would be succeeded by his brother James, Duke of York, who married the Catholic Mary of Modena in 1673 and 'came out' as a Catholic himself at the same time. In 1678 the Popish Plot, one of England's great moral panics, stirred anti-Catholic anxieties to fever pitch, caused several executions, and led to a three-year political campaign to exclude James from the throne. The king survived threat of Exclusion but the prospect of a Catholic king remained, unless the claims of Charles II's illegitimate but Protestant son, James, Duke of Monmouth were to be considered.

The Exclusion crisis was fought out in parliament and anxiety was intensified by the frenzied activity of three parliamentary elections within three years. The government sought to influence these elections by manipulating the charters of parliamentary boroughs, altering the criteria for voters and candidates so as to advantage their supporters. This was applied particularly to constituencies where opponents of the government were seen as powerful, such as Bridport and Lyme, which contained substantial numbers of dissenters, protestants who opposed the intolerant Anglican religious settlement of the 1660s, who worshiped separately in what were derisively termed 'conventicles', and were characterised by the Secretary of State, Sir Leoline Jenkins, as 'steeped in the dregs of disaffection'. Both had their charters called in and reissued three times between 1661 and 1688. In 1685 James II tried to win over dissenters with the offer of freedom of worship, as a means to allow Catholic worship at the same time, so local dissenters were caught between longing for the former and abhorrence of the latter. Locally, authority rested with the Justices of the Peace, whose wildly contrasting policies were perfectly shown in a letter written from Symondsbury at this time:

> 'Mr Strode of Parnham approves himself a very zealous, loyal prudent person. Finding other Dissenting preachers at Lyme, he destroyed all the seats and the pulpit of the meeting house there and at Bridport… Another justice does us a great deal of hurt, Mr Ellisdon of Charmouth, who receiving fines lately from a convicted conventicle refused to give a third to the poor of the parish and *has given it to the very preacher that was convicted* [my italics]'.

Richard Brodrepp II's political affiliations can be reconstructed only indirectly. After his grandfather's staunch support of the parliamentary opposition, in a parish where the rector was ejected in 1662 [see p. 61] and with family links with many leading local puritan families, his background is clear. In April 1685 he put himself forward as a candidate in the parliamentary election at Bridport. The constituency with about 280 electors was open to a range of influences. The powerful external presence of the royalist Strangways family at Melbury, and Sir George Strode at Parnham fresh from destroying the meeting house, was balanced by a strong dissenting party in the town itself. In February a remodelled charter had specifically strengthened the role of the local gentry like the Strodes and Strangways. A keen and ambitious Sherborne lawyer, Hugh Hodges, was installed as Recorder, and two members of the Strangways family were made burgesses. In these circumstances, it is not surprising that the court candidates including Hodges were returned, and Brodrepp's candidacy is only known by the defeated candidates' petition against the result. Brodrepp would have been called a 'Whig', the term having been minted during the Exclusion crisis to characterise (and to insult) those who sought to exclude James from the succession and some of whom at least favoured a degree of religious toleration.

The political temperature was raised further that summer by the landing of the Duke of Monmouth at Lyme Regis. The initial success and ultimate failure of this under-resourced

St Mary's, Bridport. Brass to Edward Coker, 1685.

and poorly coordinated invasion is not relevant here but the 'Protestant' Duke's first sally out of Lyme, a six mile march on Bridport, was not unsuccessful. The little force was met by the county militia which scattered when charged and two men, Wadham Strangways of Stinsford recently one of the town's MPs and Edward Coker, Gent, were killed. Brodrepp contributed to the militia; one assumes he was there on the day. His attitude to Monmouth's invasion cannot be surmised. Its crippling weaknesses was its failure to attract almost any gentry and Brodrepp may have been as hesitant as any to support a claim based on illegitimacy. Later that summer the quartered parts of ten executed Monmouth rebels decorated Bridport; more hung from the tower of Beaminster church.

Over the next three years James II's headlong attempt to introduce freedom of conscience as a means to allow Roman Catholic worship gathered momentum as it strengthened opposition. His first parliament having proved insufficiently cooperative, the king determined to call another for which the magistracy was purged, so Brodrepp was sacked as a Justice, and the charter of Bridport was again remodelled to favour only Catholics and dissenters. But it was the birth of the king's son, James (the Old Pretender), in June 1688 that proved the turning point. Now the king's policies would not end with his death and the succession of his protestant daughter Mary, married to William, Prince of Orange; they would continue indefinitely. William was invited to come to England to defend protestantism; on November 5 (Gunpowder Day) he arrived at Torbay. The substantial royal army put up no resistance and James fled throwing the Great Seal into the Thames.

A vacuum in government was filled as best it could be and writs went out for elections to a 'free' parliament, its electorate to be 'made by such persons only, as, according to ancient laws and customs ought to chose Members of Parliament'. With all recent attempts at interference thus set aside, an election took place in Bridport on 11 January. Brodrepp stood again, this time in company with a vivid London radical and both were returned.

Richard Brodrepp was perhaps fifty at this time. His efforts to enter parliament through the last few tumultuous years had been rewarded. He would go to London, mix with a wider world at a point when parliament might fulfil what appear to have been his political ideals. In fact, almost nothing happened. The parliament to which he had been elected, known as the 'Convention' Parliament because of its unconstitutional origins, lasted just a year in which it enacted major legislation such as the Bill of Rights, but Brodrepp played almost no part in it and made two applications to leave. He served on four unimportant committees. By March 1689 it was all over and he did not stand again.

If national politics proved uncongenial, whether for reasons of health or travel or unfamiliarity, expense, or disinclination, there was much at home to fill Brodrepp's final years. He had been reinstated as a JP in James II's final reversal of his previous policies in his last chaotic months on the throne, so there was the usual round of county business, riding over to Bradford Abbas with some colleagues to find out whether a broken bridge was the county's responsibility, and the endless tiny investigations of bastardy claims and the poor law. His local status brought with it involvement in the executorship of the wills of prominent or wealthy local people such as Robert Larder of Loders, Sheriff, in 1677-8. The inventory taken after his death shows that Larder had, besides land, about £9300, two thirds of which was laid out in loans – what else could be done with surplus cash in a world without banks? – but somewhere in the old house that preceded Loders Court, the appraisors found £503 worth of silver coin and 252 guineas, and there were hundreds of sheep and cattle besides. It is the largest total in any surviving Dorset inventory of the period. There seemed to be no difficulties and Brodrepp received the customary ring for his troubles.

He also became involved in the liquidation of the estate of Catholic George Penne based on Toller Whelme. Here was a ruined estate, on the wrong side of the day's politics: it had been sequestered during the Civil War, and the current owner had fought as brigadier-general at the Battle of the Boyne for James II: £7,000 was needed to pay his debts. The matter dragged on long after Brodrepp's death. In the end the estate was bought by George Richards, MP of Long Bredy, and was sold on again in 1802 by his son Rev. John Richards, grandson of Thomas Brodrepp and an important link in the inheritance of the Mapperton estate.

More complex was sorting out the charitable intentions of Frances Tucker of Beaminster. This wealthy spinster died in her forties early in 1685 and intended to set up a trust to establish a free school in Beaminster for the education of twenty of the poorest boys in the town, 'to take care of their manners, to chastise them to teach them to reade, to write and some competent manner to cast an account'. It was to be led by Brodrepp. She intended to consult her executors about the 200 good books to be distributed at her funeral, but it is not clear how far preliminary arrangements had been set up when she died. All, including many legacies to relations and others, was to be financed from the profits of farms at North Mapperton and South Mapperton worth £190 p.a. The Trustees named in the will refused to act. It is not clear in Brodrepp's case why he was unwilling to carry out a charitable intention similar to that of his grandfather's support of the Beaminster Poor House. His judgement may have been swayed by the calamitous fire in Beaminster of July 1684 just before Frances Tucker's death, in which she lost more than any other inhabitant. But he, no one more, would have known the value of her land. Over the next twenty years some of Frances Tucker's relatives did manage to get the school endowed and opened. In that process much of the farmland at North Mapperton was sold and Richard Brodrepp was its purchaser.

The North Mapperton acquisition took some years to carry through; a more immediate and important addition to the estate was made in 1695 when Brodrepp bought the estate at Melplash previously in possession of the Symes family, and once owned by the Paulets. He is said to have owned 1200 acres before these late purchases and he emerges as a substantial landowner here and with the Little Comberton, (Worcs.) estate still in his possession. Melplash was to be occupied by his younger son, Thomas Brodrepp, then a Fellow of Merton College, Oxford, who later played a significant part in the local community alongside his elder brother Richard, and whose son Richard IV (d.1774) was the last of the Brodrepps at Mapperton.

Finally, Richard Brodrepp had to choose a new vicar on the death of George Bowden in 1699. His choice fell upon a John Powell, about whose background nothing seems to be known, and of whose style of churchmanship there are few indications. He had enough money to set about building a new rectory for himself, of which his meticulous accounts survive. A site was chosen at a slight distance north west of the main house. The building cost £246.16s. 4d. The outside remains almost unaltered, but the interior has been rearranged and tiles have replaced thatch. Brodrepp's own care for his church had been shown thirty years earlier when he presented a new chalice and paten; now, in his final years, he rebuilt the nave.

Inheritance: Eighteenth Century Brodrepps

The succession to Richard Brodrepp II in 1706 was jarred by the sudden death of his oldest son and heir just two years later – just as he had himself succeeded after the untimely death of his father – so a younger son, another Richard, the third, followed at Mapperton for the next thirty years. By now the new family of a century before was well established in the county. Their father's purchases had built up the estate to well over 1,000 acres and with that went public service as Justice of the Peace which Richard III's father and grandfather had been. In this official business he was often accompanied by Bryan Combe, of South Mapperton, a rising attorney, who was appointed Deputy Clerk of the Peace in 1715, and Clerk ten years later. Proximity and professional interests encouraged closer family ties and Combe's daughter Jane was to marry Richard's nephew in 1738.

The Brodrepps' Whig politics, demonstrated in the difficult years of James II, continued into the eighteenth century. While it is not possible to establish what sort of churchmanship was practised in the church at Mapperton under the lead of the Revd. John Powell, Richard III's political allegiance continued the family tradition. Whig interest in West Dorset was weak, dominated as the area was by the Tory Strangways family at Melbury while the Whig Trenchards concentrated on the Poole constituency from their base at Lytchett Matravers. The borough of Bridport, with its independent merchants and strong dissenting tradition and where his father had so briefly been the Member of Parliament, was where Richard III first sought support. During the years 1712-16 he sought election as one of the Capital Burgesses. Initially he was unsuccessful, outvoted by a group of Strangways supporters, but by 1716 the balance of power shifted markedly in favour of the Whigs. The death of the strongly Tory Queen Anne in 1714, the arrival of King George from Hanover and the suppression of the Jacobite rebellion the following year all helped this. At the same time the Strangways candidate at Bridport had died and the family devoted its attention to the much more prestigious county seat, so Richard III reached his desired local endorsement. In the aftermath of the Jacobite rebellion of which the most dangerous part could have been the projected rising in the western counties focussed on Somerset, Richard III held the responsible position of Colonel of the County Militia.

His developing political ambitions are scantily recorded. At a by-election for the county seat of Dorsetshire caused by Thomas Strangways' death in the spring of 1727, the *London Journal* noticed that there was a 'vast appearance of Freeholders brought [to Dorchester] from the Western Parts by [Richard] Brodrepp Esq.'. This support among people he would have known personally did not prevent the election to the safe Tory seat of the young, unstable George Pitt of Stratfieldsaye. However, following the death of King George I in August six months later a general election had to be called. This time Richard III stood, not for Bridport as his father had done, but for the county seat itself where all the free holders of the county had the vote, amounting usually to about 2,400 voters. The large electorate and the status of free holders was precisely what gave the county seats their pre-eminence. Two identical copies of election 'literature' in the form of appeals by Brodrepp and Pitt for support show the labour involved in canvassing. On election day, 12 September 1727, no fewer than 4061 votes were recorded, but only about 1000 of those went to Brodrepp, while the rest went to unremarkable and unreconstructed Tories. That thousand might well have been the same freeholders he had persuaded to make the journey over to Dorchester in the previous spring, but they were not enough. He did not stand again.

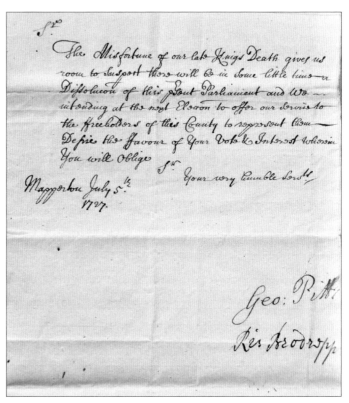

Election material, 1727. [Dorset History Centre]

When the *London Journal* picked out Richard III's contribution to the first 1727 election he was described as 'son-in-law to the Archbishop of Canterbury'. Richard's first wife Elizabeth had died in 1713 leaving two teenage daughters and in the following year he found another wife in Hester Wake, third daughter (of six) of Bishop William Wake, who in January 1716 was promoted from Lincoln to Canterbury. The Wakes were a Dorset family famous for their loyal sufferings during the Civil War, and Richard and Hester were married at her grandfather's seat at Shapwick in October, 1716. The new Archbishop was but a moderate Whig himself. A cultivated, energetic, conscientious administrator of his diocese, Wake also had patronage to bestow and in the summer of 1718 it was announced that the office of 'Register' of the Prerogative Court of Canterbury had been created for three men, Henry Seymer of Hanford, Thomas Bennett of Norton Bavant (Wilts.) and Richard Brodrepp, who just happened to be his sons-in-law. The actual work of the Prerogative Court, which handled the vast majority of wills and testamentary cases and much else at Doctors Commons below St Paul's, was of course to be handled by a deputy. It was a sufficiently happy occasion to justify a party. The *Original Weekly Journal* noted on 12 July that 'the three new Registers … gave a splendid Entertainment to most of the Doctors, Proctors Clerks, and other officers of Doctors Commons, at a Tavern near the said Commons'. Wake had no sons, and when he died in early 1737, his daughters became heiresses to his £100,000 fortune. The prospect of a part of this fortune descending upon the already wealthy Brodrepps was to affect the family in unexpected ways.

The absence of any family papers enforces reliance on public information, on local politics and administration, on fragments of gossip picked up in the London journals, or local taxes and rent payments, all of which emphasise only the male line. Even the Brodrepp family tree, as established in the late eighteenth century was designed only to show descent of the estate and any attempt to explore collaterals to reach wider ties of relationship and affection by which a family knows itself can only be incomplete. When Catherine, widow of Christopher Brodrepp (d. 1659) wrote her own will a couple of years after her husband's death she had scrupulously remembered her seven children, but also showed her affection for her sister Margaret St. Loe in her bequest 'to buy her a piece of plate in Remembrance of my love and a little picture drawn for the Remembrance of my late father'. This and an affectionate reference to her brother-in-law John links the Mapperton family with St. Loes at Fontmell Parva who were just about to build the house there, now with its bravura mid-nineteenth century additions. And when Catherine's daughter Mary died unmarried just three years later, handing on the silver cup and sugar box she had just inherited from her mother

Netherbury churchyard, chest tomb of John and Elizabeth Brodrepp, 1694.

to her sister Katherine, she too referred to her 'beloved uncle' John St Loe and made him her executor. Mary also left £50 to another uncle and aunt, John and Elizabeth Brodrepp, of Yondover, Netherbury who are commemorated in a handsome tomb in the churchyard there. One of their children became Rector of Chesilbourne and Prebendary of Norwich. Another connection was established with the widespread Freke family of Iwerne Courtney when Richard II's younger brother John married Elizabeth Freke in 1653. Further kindred are shown when a John Freke died suddenly at his house in Red Lion Square in 1717 leaving the residue of his estate to his 'sister', one Ann Brodrepp. When she died she left two daughters Ann and Mary comfortably off. Ann married the squire of Great Gaddesden (Herts), Henshaw Halsey, who in his will of 1738 loaded her with possessions. These included 'a Silver tea Kettle which was given her by her sister Mrs Mary Brodrepp soon after our marriage'. He had also left her a house in Red Lion Square, but a codicil shows that it had already been sold so instead he gave her all its remaining furniture and 'particularly her picture and my picture and my sister Brodrepps picture drawn by Jarvis [Charles Jarvis, 1675-1739] and her uncles picture by Ryley [John Riley 1646-1691] and my own done by Zinks [Christian F. Zincke, c.1684-1767]'. It is only when the other sister, Mary, wrote her will in her house in fashionable Upper Brook Street, Grosvenor Square in 1779, that the connection of these women with the Mapperton family becomes apparent.

Whether it was 'one gowne & petticoat' worth £2 6s. that Ann Symes of Mapperton had to bequeath 1631, or 'my own and my Brother Halsey's Picture set round with diamonds' that Mary Brodrepp would eventually hand on in 1779, together with 'all the China on the Mantlepiece in my parlour and the two pair of old blue and white China Basons', women bequeathed their personal possessions because that alone was within their legal ownership; land, including whatever they themselves might have brought to a marriage, was almost always men's business. Richard Brodrepp II (d. 1708) and his son Robert two years later created an entail for the substantial estate of which Mapperton was the centre, to descend successively to his brothers and to their sons down to the seventh son and their heirs and then to any daughters and their heirs. Thus the estate's future integrity was ring-fenced, always in the expectation of a ready supply of heirs.

Richard III's marriage with Hester Wake was duly successful in the birth of a son, George in 1715. When he progressed to University College, Oxford, in 1733 his social standing was strongly asserted by his appearance among the orators in the last University 'Act', the extended summer festival set up very occasionally – this was the first for 22 years – for the awarding of honorary degrees. It has now been succeeded by the annual Encaenia. The 1733 Act is remembered now as an extremely busy week for Handel and his band of London musicians, supplemented by a few local performers who performed five operas and much else, but for George and perhaps his parents too, it was a spectacular summer party. As one enthusiastic undergraduate wrote home:

> 'All the lodgings in Town have been long ago bespoke for the Accomodation of
> Ge[ntle]men & Ladies, who intend to visit us. We expect mo[st] of the Nobility &
> some of the Royal Family & very great Preparations are now making.'

In the company of Lord Barry, son of Lord Barrymore, Lord Viscount Castlecomer, and Hon.

William Tracy, son of Viscount Rathcoole from his own college, George Brodrepp, Gentleman Commoner, delivered an oration in Latin lyric verse, possibly even of his own authorship, on 'The Bounty of Dr Radcliffe'. These were the years when final plans were being made for using the bequest of Dr John Radcliffe whose £40,000 fortune had been left to the University in 1714. The first stone for the Radcliffe Library was laid in June 1737.

George Brodrepp entered into his inheritance when his father died the following October leaving a simple will that bequeathed almost everything to him. His prospects interested the University of Oxford sufficiently for the *Daily Post* to record that 'George Brodrepp of University College, Grandson to the late Archbishop of Canterbury,' was awarded an honorary Degree of Master of Arts by the University. The death of Archbishop Wake the previous January had meant that George's mother Hester would inherit a substantial legacy. Clearly now, George, a 'single man in possession of a good fortune, must be in want of a wife'. In fact, in February 1739 it was his mother Hester who remarried. She married Thomas, the younger brother of George Strode who from 1727 had succeeded to Parnham. Links to the Strodes of Parnham were already close. Catherine Brodrepp, George Brodrepp's oldest half-sister had married Hugh Strode, a London merchant, in 1720 and following his death less than two years later, she had married his first cousin George, of Parnham in 1728. Now Hester was married to George's younger brother Thomas. Catherine would have been in residence at Parnham, when in the country, from the late 1720s, and her step-mother would most likely live in London.

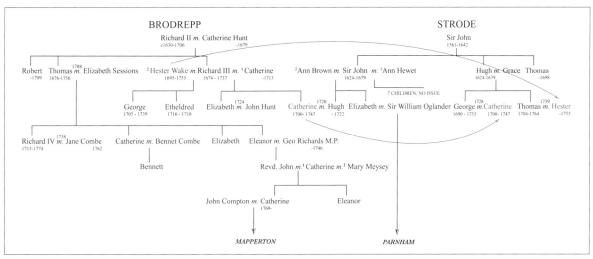

Family Tree illustrating intermarriage of Brodrepp and Strode Families

Nothing sheds light on this sudden step but, of the (few) notices in London papers that refer to any event at Mapperton, this marriage and its speed attracted most attention, being repeated nine times in the capital and even in provincial papers. The Strodes could be seen as avaricious fortune hunters, eager to snatch a passing fortune or even a neighbouring estate, or they could be old friends offering solace. The fierce avidity of the mid eighteenth century marriage market, with its relentless and much-referenced search for heiresses implied by the newspaper reaction to the remarriage of Hester Brodrepp to Thomas Strode, is set out with chilling clarity in *The Master-Key to the Rich Ladies Treasury, Or the Widower and Bachelor's Directory of 1742*. This is nothing more than a list of possible heiresses in order of rank starting with dowager duchesses, giving the size of their fortunes and, in the case of the majority, a London address. Among 'Spinsters' a Miss Brodrepp is listed, with a reputed fortune of £10,000 in stocks. This probably refers to Mary Brodrepp, collecting her ceramics in Upper Brook Street, and subscribing to improving sermons.

In November 1739, just thirteen months after his father, the twenty-four year old George Brodrepp died. The direct male line of the family came to an end, and succession to the estate passed to George's uncle Thomas, Richard III's younger brother. For a moment no one had need of the house at Mapperton with Hester in London and Thomas Brodrepp well established only a short walk away. Two melancholy sales took place. The first disposed of 'A compleat set of Black Coach Geldings . . and if desir'd, a handsome Chariot …that were new last summer, and have been very little used'. The second the following year saw the dispersal of the rest of George's possessions – 'Household Furniture, Plate, China, Books Linen, Chariot and Implements of Husbandry'.

Two significant church monuments offer some commentary on these complex family rearrangements. Soon after the death of Richard III in 1737, Hester Brodrepp commissioned a monument for him to be installed at Mapperton. She chose the Flemish sculptor Peter Scheemakers, who had studied in Rome and made his name on his arrival in London in *c.*1720 with the carving of the huge monument to the Duke of Buckingham in Westminster Abbey. A design for the Brodrepp monument shows a flat plinth carrying the inscription upon which

P. Scheemakers' design for Brodrepp Monument, c.1737.
© Victoria & Albert Museum, London D.1040-1887.

All Saints, Mapperton. Monument to Richard Brodrepp, 1739.

a tall obelisk in dark marble provides the background for two putti surrounding the draped oval relief of his portrait. The most influential model of this type was Rysbrack's monument to the poet John Gay, just unveiled in the Abbey in April 1737. The monument as it stands at Mapperton differs from the surviving drawing by the inclusion, high up on the obelisk, of a small niche containing a frontal head of George, so it was clearly not erected before his death in 1739. The role of Hester, now Strode, 'One of the Daughters and Coheiresses of Dr. Wm. Wake late Arch Bishop of Canterbury' is prominent on the inscription of this monument that commemorates her husband, her son George, and a daughter, named Etheldred for her grandmother, who had died as a child twenty years before. It probably cost about £140.

Head of George Brodrepp on his father's monument.

The second monument was erected in Beaminster in *c*.1754 pursuant to the will of George Strode, the second husband of Catherine Brodrepp who had died eight years earlier. George set aside a sum 'not to exceed six hundred pounds or less than five hundred pounds' for a monument 'in memory of me and my dear wife', and charged his executor with the responsibility. This was his younger brother, Thomas, by then married to Hester (Wake) whose choice of sculptor a few years before may have been influential now. Husband and wife are depicted in the grand manner, recumbent in white marble on a sarcophagus,

contrasting with the grey obelisk behind them. On either side stand two allegorical figures of Hope and Charity, suggesting that the third female, Hester herself, shown pointing her husband's attention toward a book in a manner Scheemakers had employed elsewhere, was Faith. There is no way of knowing to what extent

a portrait was attempted. The brief inscription refers to Catherine as 'one of the daughters and coheiresses of Richard Brodrepp, late of Mapperton'. It is not clear to what extent Catherine had been an heiress. Her father's will did not interfere with the

St Mary's Beaminster, Monument to George Strode, 1753.

Head of Catherine Brodrepp on Strode monument.

strict settlement of the estate made by his own father; in which Catherine received just £50 for mourning. She was more obviously an heiress on account of her previous marriage to Hugh Strode, the London merchant who had given her the manor of Seaborough, Dorset. The monument makes no reference to children. Catherine (Brodrepp) had no children by either of her husbands, and neither did Hester with Thomas Strode. He was the last Strode to live at Parnham which passed on his death to the family of his sister's husband, Sir William Oglander, of the Isle of Wight. Many eighteenth-century monuments were erected deliberately to mark the ending of a line; neither of these do so explicitly but, in their different ways, both mark a lack of heirs.

It is unlikely that Mapperton stood empty for long after the death of George Brodrepp in the winter of 1739. His cousin Richard had just married and Thomas Brodrepp to whom the estate was entailed probably made the house over to his son. Dr. Thomas Brodrepp MD was the last survivor of Richard Brodrepp II's children. Born in 1676, he had been Fellow of Merton College, Oxford, then lived at Melplash Court and played an active part in local life both as a magistrate and in the development of Bridport Harbour in 1740. Of his practice as a physician only one incident is recorded, part of the ongoing public discussion of the merits of inoculation against smallpox. In 1746 the physician at St Bartholomew's Hospital, Pierce Dod MD, a strong opponent of inoculation, published a pamphlet in which he quoted Thomas Brodrepp 'a learned and experienced Physician in those parts', who had supplied evidence that a young lad who had been inoculated and then caught smallpox a couple of years later. Dod used this one case as evidence of the inefficacy of inoculation. Thomas Brodrepp's own opinions on inoculation at that early period before even Benjamin Jesty's experiments at Yetminster, are not entirely clear from this, but the anecdote is of some relevance because the boy in question was Brodrepp's own grandson, John Richards, later Rector of Litton Cheney, who himself played a part in the descent of the Mapperton estate.

Thomas had married in 1706 and four of his children reached adulthood. All married into families in the immediate locality, there being little likelihood while their cousin George was alive of their succeeding to the Mapperton estate. The first was Catherine (referred to by the *Weekly Miscellany* as Kitty) who in 1735 was married in London to Bennet Combe, a nephew of the Mapperton lawyer, and she was followed by Eleanor, described by the *Grub Street Journal* as 'a lady of great beauty, merit and fortune', who married George Richards of Long Bredy, soon to be MP for Bridport, in 1737. During 1738 Thomas Brodrepp's only son Richard married Bryan Combe's daughter Jane, while another daughter married William Light of Baglake, Litton Cheney. All but the last would be involved in the succession to the Mapperton estate.

Richard IV (1710-74) was to live at Mapperton for forty-five years. Admitted to the Middle Temple in 1728, he had read for the bar, and practised as a barrister until 1757. He also continued his predecessors' active role in local government. At one point he was a Deputy Lieutenant as his grandfather had been, chairman of the Bridport justices and Recorder for the town. From this established position, a seat in Parliament could be the next step. The county seats appeared to be safe in Tory hands, yet commentators agreed that if only the Whigs could unite themselves they were theirs for the taking, indeed George Dodington of Eastbury reckoned that two thirds of the property in the county was in Whig hands. As Henry Fox remarked to his nephew the sickly Lord Digby, who was considering standing in 1753, 'If you don't decline, you'll certainly carry it, but whether at an expense at all worth while God knows'. So, in 1765 when it appeared that there would be a by-election for the county seat, the Earl of Shaftesbury, Lord Lieutenant and the leading Whig magnate in the county, sounded Brodrepp out:

> 'I wrote to our most valuable Friend Mr Brodrepp to acquaint him with [the possible by-election] and beg his assistance. At the same time taking the liberty to affirm what Mr Brodrepp knows to be true That if he would accept being a County Member, he must be certain of an Unanimous Election. But as he has more than once declined coming into Parliament, and I have reason to fear he will preserve in the same resolution, I told him that we ought to take our measures accordingly.'

Some reserve inhibited Brodrepp, although he may have found it difficult to come out as a supporter of the chilly Prime Minister, George Grenville and his increasingly unpopular administration, at that time imposing the Stamp Act on the American colonies.

Five owners of Mapperton have been tempted by a seat in the House of Commons. Richard II seems to have been disenchanted on the briefest acquaintance, Richard III failed election; Richard IV would not stand. In 1905 Henry Francis Compton had the misfortune to be elected to support a government that resigned two days before his poll and then a general election was called a few days later so that, though successful, he never took his seat. By these standards, Victor Montagu's twenty-one year tenure of the South Dorset seat, even with its unwished-for ending, was achievement and stability itself.

Richard IV's life lies tantalisingly just out of reach. The tiny scrap of paper that shows him buying stained glass for

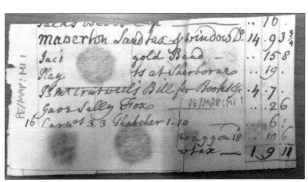

Fragment of account book of Richard Brodrepp IV.
[Dorset History Centre]

the church in 1768 comes from a meticulous account book which, if kept over years would vividly illustrate his tastes. As it is, two entries for 'Play Tickets at Sherborne . . 19s.' and 'Pd. Mr Cruttwell's Bill for Books &c £4.7s.' shows him in touch with a lively cultural environment. The little town of Sherborne (population 2-3,000) boasted two newspapers, of which the *Sherborne Journal* had just been set up by William Cruttwell (1741-1804) as a rival to the older *Sherborne Mercury*. As for the theatre, George Tatham's research shows that a few months earlier he might have attended Dryden's *Cato* 'acted by the gentlemen of the free grammar school'. This had enjoyed 'very crowded audiences of the principal inhabitants of the town and the Gentry of the neighbourhood for some miles around and gave universal satisfaction'. In 1769 the same troupe put on the *Eunuch* of Terence, but what was on in the winter season in 1768 is not known. The other side of the scrap from the account book shows Brodrepp in London where he purchased the church glass, spending £1.1s. on 'Pamphlets & Print'. Books were clearly a major interest; he subscribed to books on farming and on topography, of which the most notable was Hutchins's *History of Dorset* for which he was down for four copies. He will have known of the book because of Hutchins's own

visits to Mapperton, and his patronage is recognised in a cartouche on the map of Bridport, although it is not clear whether he ever saw the volumes for they were published only months before his death. After Brodrepp's death his library, advertised as 'the curious Law Library of the late Counsellor Broderip

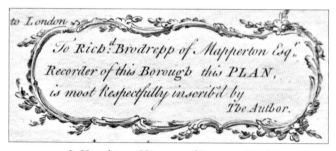

J. Hutchins, History of Dorset 1774; cartouche on map of Bridport.

of Mapperton' was sold by the Exeter bookseller, Edward Score. Even less well documented is his patronage of painters. An inscription on the back of the portrait of his Rector's son, to the effect that Brodrepp provided the boy with a cocked hat for the portrait, probably

Mapperton, North front.

by Thomas Beach, suggests a visit by the painter to Mapperton and his own interested participation in the business [see page 62]. It is hard to believe that he would not also have had his own portrait taken.

Brodrepp's principal impact at Mapperton was the reconstruction of the north facade. A two storey staircase hall was created slightly off centre, so that the sixteenth-century plaster ceiling of the drawing room was undamaged. New plaster ceilings were installed in the hall itself and the Library. The walls were panelled, shielding the rare sixteenth-century overmantels to be rediscovered at the beginning of the twentieth century. The exterior elevation was brought up to date with rectangular sash windows either side of a simple pedimented doorway. This was a conservative intervention leaving intact much old-fashioned decoration. It has been attributed to the Bastard family; by the 1740s when Richard IV may have been considering building work, there were five members of the family operating from Sherborne

Mapperton, library ceiling c. 1750.

as well as Blandford who might have been responsible, and craftsmen, whether plasterers, woodcarvers or staircase builders, may have acted independently.

Mapperton, Detail of Chimneypiece formerly in Drawing Room

Perhaps this partial rebuilding was in expectation of a family, but the marriage to Jane Combe yielded no children, and when she died in May 1762 Richard, over fifty, did not marry again. His will written within

a fortnight of his own death in 1774 distributed his wealth among his own siblings and their children, and the siblings of his late wife Jane. Apart from one sister, Eleanor Richards of Long Bredy who survived him by just a year, the principal beneficiaries were the two men to whom the estate was most likely to pass. To one nephew, Revd. John Richards, Rector of Litton Cheney and Eleanor's only surviving son, he bequeathed the huge sum of £10,000, but the residue of his goods and his entire estate went to Bennet Combe of Lincoln's Inn, son of his sister Catherine. Little is known of Bennet Combe; it is not clear that he ever occupied the house. It is ironic that it is his name that was adopted by the Compton family in acknowledgement of an estate of which he was merely the most recent possessor. Combe's will was written only four months after his uncle Richard's although it was not fully settled till 1806. His entire estate, so recently enlarged by his uncle's bequest, passed to Eleanor and

Catherine, the daughters of Revd. John Richards of Litton Cheney, who in 1774 were not yet ten, and by the time these heiresses were ready for marriage Eleanor had died so that it was Catherine who was to carry the Mapperton estate to its new owner. But already from the time of Richard IV's death, John Richards' daughters were heiresses to his £10,000, his estates at Long Bredy, Toller Whelme and much else. No time was lost in snapping up such an heiress: at St. James's, Piccadilly, on 24 March 1788, Catherine Richards, minor, 'of this parish' [not in fact, but of the neighbouring parish of St Marylebone where Revd. James Richards had a house in Queen Anne St. East,] was married to John Compton 'with the consent of the Revd. John Richards, clerk, natural and lawful father of the said minor by License from the Archbishop of Canterbury, 24 March 1788'. The Comptons were a junior branch of the family that in Tudor times had been created Earls of Northampton, and which had been seated at Minstead, Hants. since the sixteenth century. There can have been no question but that the young bride would leave behind an estate where she had never lived to begin her married life in Hampshire. And so Mapperton was put into the hands of the Rector's brother, the Beaminster attorney Baruch Fox, who inserted the following advertisement in the London newspapers.

London Evening Post, 6 April 1775.

III

The People on the Land

It should be clear that the Morgan-Brodrepp estate based on the house at Mapperton had always been much larger than just the parish. The original Devon manor of Morgan Hayes may have gone with a daughter's marriage into the Rose family in the mid-seventeenth century and the Worcestershire lands were sold in 1748, but they continued to own ancestral land at Huntspill and at Burnham in Somerset. In addition there remained farms in Uploders, Allington and Broadwindsor, Marnhull and a considerable estate at Melplash. This chapter attempts to look outside the big house and to catch sight where possible of Mapperton's other inhabitants.

The census of 1881 gives the population of the parish of Mapperton as 120, which may be the highest it ever reached. In the mid-eighteenth century Hutchins reckoned it had fifty souls; before that, in about 1600, the vicar stated there were fifty communicants, so the total population then would have exceeded a hundred. At that moment of maximum population in 1881, twenty-four houses were occupied and the average age of the inhabitants was just over twenty-six. The hundred and twenty were not all in one location, but distributed in the three distinct settlements that had characterised the parish since medieval times. Apart from Mapperton itself there was Coltleigh on its hill to the north-east, and Mythe where the streams met in the valley. The big house was occupied in 1881 by an adult family of three with three servants.

The earliest it is possible to know of individual people in the parish occurs towards the end of the sixteenth century. From the 1570s through to 1640 a fortunate combination of surviving records throws sharp if fitful light on the lives of some of Mapperton's inhabitants. Although the parish register of christenings, marriages and burials is lost, a handful of wills and inventories are supplemented by the presentments to the Dean of Sarum about the condition of the church (and of the new rector), and to these are added for some years the proceedings of the manorial court, and a few of the tenants' presentments to it. The very latest is a letter of 1640 from the lord of the manor Richard Brodrepp I to a Bridport attorney seeking his attendance at the manorial court. It is the only letter of his to survive and it expresses the courteous care with which he took his local responsibilities, as his activity on the County Committee has shown.

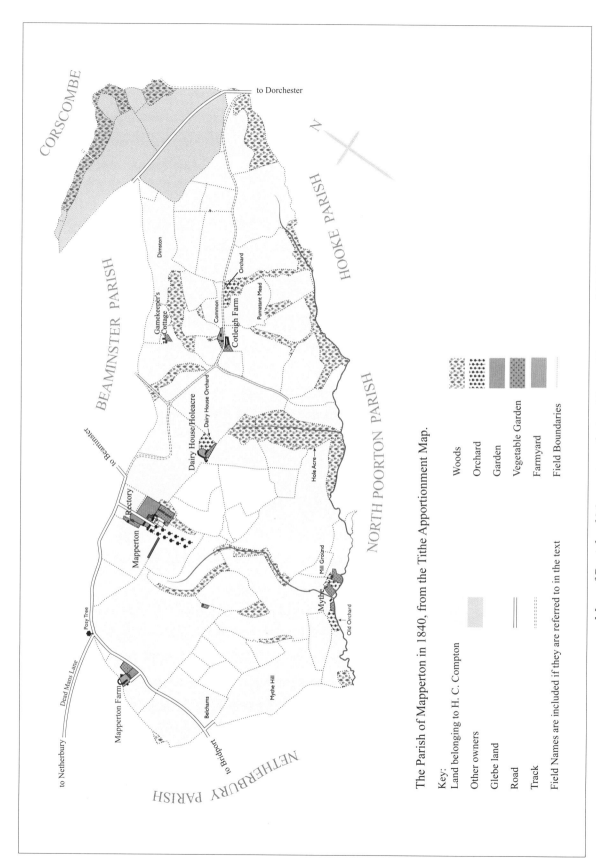

The Parish of Mapperton in 1840, from the Tithe Apportionment Map.

Key:
Land belonging to H. C. Compton

Other owners

Glebe land

Road

Track

Field Names are included if they are referred to in the text

Woods

Orchard

Garden

Vegetable Garden

Farmyard

Field Boundaries

Map of Parish of Mapperton, derived from tithe map of 1840.

CORSCOMBE

BEAMINSTER PARISH

HOOKE PARISH

NORTH POORTON PARISH

NETHERBURY PARISH

to Dorchester

to Beaminster

to Netherbury

to Bridport

Dead Mans Lane

Posy Tree

Mapperton Farm

Belchams

Mythe Hill

Mythe

Old Orchard

Mill Ground

Hole Acre

Mapperton

Rectory

Dairy House/Holeacre

Dairy House Orchard

Gamekeeper's Cottage

Dimston

Common

Cotleigh Farm

Orchard

Pumatant Mead

N

42

Mr Loder, I present to you and yo.r good wife the hearty salutacions of me and myne

And doe entreat you so to sett yr. occasions that you may be att Map(er)to(n) to keep a

Court for me there the Tenth day of this Aprill, against wch tymes also to make ready

John Birt's Copy [a Copyhold lease, for three lives] … yor loving frend. Ri Brodrepp.

The late sixteenth century was a time of quickly rising population, when the pressures of inflation placed new strains on the customary relationships between manorial lord and his tenants. More fortunate tenants by now enjoyed some security of tenure through the practice of copyhold tenancy whereby a family might be able to stay on the same land for three generations, but Tudor inflation put landowners under pressure to increase incomes and to contest customs that tenants had got used to in the centuries since the Black Death had given them advantage in the labour market. Early in Elizabeth's reign a document dating from the reign of Richard II listing 'Customs of the Manor' of Mapperton was rediscovered and copied, itemising the works due to the lord. The only person with an interest to do this would have been the lord of the manor, Robert Morgan, anxious to find out what rights might be there to contest or to reimpose. Modern historians see the making of these manorial surveys, whether retrospective like the Mapperton example, or novel by means of obtaining new maps, as the ways in which, as Andy Wood has written, 'states and elites inscribe their authority upon the environment and seek to instruct their subject populations in the reading of that environment'. We have no evidence of whether Robert Morgan's study of ancient labour obligations achieved anything at Mapperton; his early seventeenth century successor, Richard Brodrepp, appears to have been a well-intentioned and conscientious lord. Copyhold tenure certainly continued, while court records show the tenants often stating the customs of the manor, more for their mutual convenience than in any confrontation with their lord.

Coltleigh

Consisting now of a single old house, itself rebuilt in 1787, Coltleigh is the best documented of the Mapperton settlements in the early modern period. The Munden family who were its principal tenants and perhaps occupied the site of the present house, can be traced through several generations between 1525 and 1706 but as most of the men were called either John or Hugh a family tree is impossible to reconstruct. The earliest to emerge in any detail is John, father of the Catholic martyr, whose will of 1572 mentions several family members. His son Oliver was no doubt to inherit his copyhold, though the will only mentioned iron yokes for four oxen for him, while 'My best tenor sawe and the custody and keeping up of my best hand saw' were to go to a nephew 'John the carpenter'. His second biggest pan was to go to his

Coltleigh, distant view from the south.

daughter Kate, and a russet coat to his servant Richard Beele. John Munden called himself 'theldest' in his will. As a young man half a century earlier he had been assessed in Henry VIII's military survey, designed to find out what weapons were available in the countryside where he was liable for a bow and half a sheaf of arrows. When his son Oliver died in 1594 his possessions included a 'bowe and arrows sord dagger and headpiece' worth 13s. Perhaps that bow had been his father's. Oliver's brother, the John that stayed at home, served as churchwarden after his father. One year he and John Travis presented that the stair to the tower was faulty and, perennial problem, that the church's lead covering had been taken away 'by some we knowe not'.

The family did not see themselves yeomen, but only husbandmen; apart from livestock, simple house furniture and metal items of many sorts, their only wealth consisted of a few silver spoons, the most common form of usable wealth. John, senior had none; John junior distributed his carefully among his three sons. When Hugh Munden died a generation later in 1627 he left seven silver spoons 'whereof 3 broken & the rest small' weighing seven ounces and worth 33s. With this tiny resource of ready money went an assortment of brass pans and pewter platters. It was enough to raise the family above their fellow villagers, like William Cake also of Coltleigh, the bulk of whose implements were (still) made of wood.

A comparison of two Coltleigh farmers at the end of Elizabeth's reign pinpoints the slight gradations of wealth between them. Oliver Munden who succeeded his father John at Coltleigh and died in 1594 farmed the family lands held from Robert Morgan. On it he had livestock: two oxen, two cows, three bullocks and 80 sheep worth £13.7s. 8d., rather less than one third of his total estate. Most of the rest and much of the contents of his cottage consisted of a wide variety of implements for the storing, preparing and cooking of food.

Perhaps in some open space in the barton [farmyard] would have been kept the four barrels worth 3s 8d., four trendles [probably a rounded flat vessel] worth 4s., and three cheese vats, with other containers worth 3s.4d.. In the kitchen were 'Three Brasse pannes two pots wth. a Caldron 46s. 8d' and '3 Candlesticks & two salts wth. two saucers' worth 3s.8d. Otherwise, his possessions consisted of bedding: a feather bed, a flock bed, two feather bolsters and two pillows worth 40s, also three coverlets and two pairs of blankets, – essential on that windy hill, 'two pairs of sheets and two 'bord Coth' all worth 13s.4d. Apart from beds there was little furniture: '2 coffers', and downstairs 'one table board one Cobard'. Oliver's total wealth, as assessed by his neighbours, was £30. 15s. 10d..

Roger Knight died in 1603 a couple of months after Queen Elizabeth. His inventory was appraised at half as much again as Oliver Munden's, at just over £46, and the difference is marked. His four oxen were worth £10.10s; he had nine calves, a black horse and a black mare and two colts, and 3 pigs but surprisingly no sheep. He was also involved in arable farming: half an acre of barley ('more or lesse') worth 10s.; seven acres of rye, barley, oats, beans on the glebe land of the parsonage. The parsonage glebe was dotted around the parish, so this land can not be precisely located. Knight also had wood and timber at somewhere called Rudde Meadowe, which might not have been in the parish at all and also on 'mr Preston's lands' worth £8. At a house there he stored '200 of lathes, a payre of truckle wheels and ten plancks in the flore' worth 7s 6d. Agricultural production involved well over half his estate. 'In the house at Coltly' on the other hand, his furniture was very similar to Oliver Munden's: 'a table forme and Cupboard at 30s; a bedstead, Corde, bede, bolster & pillow worth 8s.4d.; a doublet, two pair of sheets at 8s. 4d., and a chest and a coffer worth 7s.'. Knight, too, had '3 brazen candlesticks and a pewter salt' worth 7s, but also '2 drinking Cupps, one of stone the other pewter & a pewter bottle – 4s'. More productively there was a cheese rack and 34 cheeses worth 16d. Knight was also growing hemp, though it is not clear where. In the Subsidy taxation list of 1594, Roger Knight is referred to a 'gent' (while John Luttrell, then occupying the main house through his marriage to Christopher Morgan's widow, was an Esquire), but at £46, neither he nor his possessions were far advanced towards gentle status.

A completely different view into the Coltleigh community in that last Elizabethan decade is given by the presentments at the Dean's visitation which took place in the summer of most years. As explained on page 13, churchwardens and sidesmen were obliged to provide answers to a series of questions about the state of the church building, on the conduct of services within it, but also to enquiries concerning the moral life of the parishioners that fell within the scope of the church courts. As churchwardens, Munden and Knight were both closely involved. In 1582 Munden reported that 'Mary Webb did confess that henry Tryvett hath had carnell copulacyon with her' but the sentence continues blithely 'all things else in good order as far as we knowe.' Perhaps nothing came of it. When a 'base child' was actually born, things might be more uncertain: 'Willm dowche is accused by one Jane dowche of porton to be the father of a child of her begotten in bastardie, but in the birth of the child she did accuse one John Lackins of porton' so perhaps it was not Mapperton's problem after all. The following year John Trevis of Mapperton was said, 'as the fame goeth', to have committed 'fornicacon' with Jone Abbot the wife of [*blank*]Abbot of Whitchurch, though what the Dean of Salisbury was expected or willing to do with such dubious evidence is unclear. However, that rumour may be connected with an incident much closer to home a few months later when 'Syselye travys the wife of John travys' was presented for

> 'gevinge of a blowe in the church yarde of maperton the ix daye of desember Immedyatlye after morninge prayer uppon Rychard wyatt the sayed wyatt beinge one of the syde men [sidesmen] and As she was aboute to strike a gayne the tethinge man [a Tithingman was nominally responsible for the behaviour of people within his area] saved him of another blowe'.

This presentment was supported by as many as six witnesses 'wyth others'. The victim, Richard Wyatt, later to be churchwarden, had just been presented himself because he 'hath suffered his mill to grind on the saboth day'. Any sense that Wyatt had had to give in to pressure to allow his mill to break the sabbath is lessened when we read some years later that 'Alice wiate widowe' was presented for profaning the Saboth in the same way, 'usuallie'. And she was to be followed in the 1630s by Robert Dogood, miller, doing the same thing 'sometimes… after evening prayer'.

Another responsibility of the churchwardens was to present those who did not come to church. In the late sixteenth century this meant recusant Catholics who could be fined for their absence. John Munden's wife Alice was repeatedly presented from the early 1590s when the wardens admitted she was 'excommunicate for we know not how long'. The Barretts, relatives of the Mundens were also presented because Mary Barrett refused to let her daughters Tamasin and Sisely attend church. In 1598 things had become so difficult with her that she was ejected from her house for a few months, though it seems to have done no good. Edith Barrett was another problem and one which the new puritan rector George Bowden was happy to pursue, writing to the Dean within months of his installation:

> Mr deane for asmuch as there is one Edith Barret an obstinate papist dwelling wthin the p(ar)ishe of map(er)ton wthin yr peculiar, who by the space of these sixteen yeares & upwards hath refused to come to anie Churche, or to receave Communion,

...& standing excomunicated in yor Courte of longe tyme & doth much hurte by her ill example in the place wheare she livethe ... not Doubting of yor godlie care for thadvancement of gods glorie & suppressinge of Idolatrie we Comit you to the grace of god

Bowden made sure to send this letter from Parnham where he got it signed by Robert Strode and John Luttrrell, gentlemen he knew would support his action, but by no other parishioners. As time went on however the generation loyal to the old religion passed and the congregation became accustomed to the new ways. A presentment of 1634 recorded the extent of this change: 'we [have not] any Recusants dwelling or living within our p(ar)ish for the space of 30 yeeres last past'.

The proceedings of the manor court show another aspect of the village community. The court's principal function was to validate land tenure, most often the succession of family members according to the terms of copyhold. Annual rent was a matter of shillings, but the fine on entering into the property by each successor could be as much as £100. Further court business resulted from widows claiming the right to succeed to their husband's tenement. By contrast, if anyone tried to sub-let their tenement they would be fined. All was done with formality in this intimate society: in 1608 on the death of John fford, tenant of Longhaies, of 40 acres, a heriot [the fine charged on a new tenant on succeeding to a property, generally of the 'best beast'] of £3 was levied. 'They were duly admitted as tenants and the said Oliver gave fealty to the Lord'. When such an arrangement was agreed to in the presence of the parties, and the lord or his steward, and of principal tenants assembled there as the 'Homage' or jury, the entry in the court roll ends 'Et fecit Dno. fidelitatem' *And he gave fealty to the Lord*. This was explained at the time:

'in doing homage the tenant kneeles in doing fealtie hee standes. In doing homage the tenant must remayne [with his head]covered, in doing fealtie he may remayne covered[.] In doing homage the Lord kisseth his tennaunt in doing fealtye he kisseth him not. Lastlie in doinge homage the tennant promiseth to become the Lordes man for life . . In doing fealtie hee sweares onelie to become the Lords faithfull tennant.

Besides the inheritance of property, the manor court attempted to regulate farming practice. Stating an intention: 'wee present that noe Tenant of Coltley shall suffer any pigg or pigge to go abroad from May day until Michaelmas' was one thing; ensuring obedience was another, and fines were levied. Wandering cattle, sheep, even John Roper's geese all presented the same problem. One of the many John Mundens was among those fined 3s. 4d. for keeping a 'horse beast' on the common at Coltleigh. The frequent reference to a 'Common' at Coltleigh in the 1630s suggests that common land still provided a useful asset, at the very same time that the churchwardens were assuring the Dean of Sarum that, although they no longer went on a perambulation of the parish boundary, 'the bounds of the parish are well known, and lands all enclosed'. Rights villagers were anxious to continue included the right to 'shrowd, top & lop, all such trees as are growing upon our several Tenements, in hedgerowes, Lantalles & Meadows'. Timber was precious commodity: John Symes was going too far in 1637 in cutting down two trees 'contrarie to the Custome of the Manor', so he was fined 6s.8d. and Henry Crabb paid 3s.4d for using trees without the Lord's permission to repair his own house.

The families that feature in the proceedings of the Manor Court are almost all among the wealthiest in the parish. They had the security of copyhold tenure; they can afford the steep £60 to £100 entry fine on inheriting such properties; they supply churchwardens and sidesmen. Beneath them are the invisibles, the landless transient population moving from one parish to another in search of work. Some may manage to scramble up into becoming sub-tenants, although the Court constantly tried to stop the practice. A measure of the proportion of Mapperton's population beneath this level is suggested at the time of the Hearth Tax of 1664, when being able to pay the tax at all is taken as a reasonable measure of wealth, though this varied widely. At Mapperton, nineteen householders were registered for the tax, from Richard Brodrepp with his ten hearths down to five men and Julian Roper, widow, who paid for one. The Dorset median of non-payers is 34%, but at North Poorton next door a few years later 78% did not pay the tax. Perhaps half of Mapperton's population in this period fell below this threshold and thus remain completely unrecorded. They might have been recorded in one other source, for the Elizabethan poor laws created a civil responsibility on each parish to raise money for the care of its own poor and also to return any vagrant poor back to their own parish. Almost no accounts of Mapperton's Overseers of the Poor have survived. Just a few pages crop up, decades later and jumbled in the parish register of christenings, marriages and burials. They provide one example of the parish looking after its poorest, paying out 1s. a week to 'ye widdow Minterne' for eight months, three weeks, and then 'A shroud for Ann Minterne, 4s.' and 'funerall expenses 10s.6d.', then a further 6d. for burial.

The longest surviving name in the village was Roper, a reference to the traditional local industry, and the earliest Roper in Mapperton was mentioned in 1341. In this period a sequence of John Ropers feature in many records; 'he' often led the Homage of the tenants to the Lord at the start of the court. In 1595-99 his house was falling down for want of timber; in 1638 he or his son was fined for keeping a couple of horses on the common and fetching them away at night, and a year later he was letting his pigs roam there. But this member of the family was also churchwarden, and as such one tiny relic of him can be found in the church. A piece of wood, evidently taken from an old pew or roof work has been fixed to the pew on

All Saints, Mapperton, fragment of earlier woodwork in chancel.

the north side of the choir bearing, as was customary, the churchwarden's initials and the date.

The present house at Coltleigh carries the date 1787 and appears to have been rebuilt when William Fry was the tenant. In the nineteenth century censuses show it among a community of about four houses, with the farm generally of about 200 acres. Tenant farmers were likely to stay in one place for longer than landless agricultural workers, who were always at the mercy of hiring fairs and annual contracts, if they were lucky. In 1827 the farm had been taken over by the young Absalom Chick, at the start of a career that ended with him farming 800 acres in Askerswell and employing twenty men. Chick moved on to be followed by the Whittle family who were at Coltleigh for twenty years and then Guy Bugler was there from *c.*1891 to his death in 1916. In 1940 when the nine year old George Brown moved there with his family, three empty cottages stood opposite the remaining farmhouse, and he remembers seeing the foundations of more cottages a couple of hundred yards further along the track. The farmhouse survives amid the outlines of the farm buildings shown on the Title Apportionment Map, but it ceased to be a working farm on George Brown's retirement in 1990. That last generation of farmers recalls a vanished plague: rabbits. George Brown remembers shooting 1,000 in a year. Dick Berry at Marsh Farm wrote, of the same period: 'It was nothing at the end of the day [harvesting] to catch between fifty to eighty rabbits in the middle of the field'. But rabbits were also a source of income to the farmer, 'and in those days very often paying the rent'.

Halfway down the hill from Coltleigh towards Mapperton stands Holeacre, formerly the Dairy House. The name first occurs in 1608 when John fford als Symes was fined 3s.4d. for cutting down trees in 'Holn acre' ['holn' = holly], the woodland below the house. The present building is said to be late seventeenth century and has been little altered. Built of substantial dressed stone, the south front is unusual in placing the original front door to the left end of the elevation, with a continuous hood mould running along above the two windows beside it. The north side retains the long passage

Holeacre, formerly Dairy House.

49

of the dairy, with cheese lofts above. In 1840 it was known as the Dairy House. The common custom was for the dairy herd to be leased out to a youngish farmer for whom managing the dairy herd from a landowner was a step on the way to a full farm tenancy. As Arthur Young pointed out on his visit to Mapperton in 1771, having the chance of a house of one's own, however briefly, as the manager of the dairy herd, brought other advantages such as the use of the farm yard to raise one's own pigs. The critical judgement lay in estimating accurately what profit could be made on raising the cattle: Young says they would be leased at £4 each, and the profit, after a year would be £6.

In 1941 the wartime Ministry of Agriculture and Fisheries [MAF] Farm Survey shows Holeacre to have been a farm of 174 acres, almost entirely given over to a herd of 59 cattle, apart from about eight acres of barley and oats, employing two men and two horses. As such it was very slightly more heavily worked than Coltleigh where a larger acreage was pasture for a smaller herd of cattle, some poultry and a few pigs.

Marsh Farm

If Coltleigh can illuminate some aspects of life and farming practice in the early modern period, at Marsh Farm it is possible to illustrate the great turning point in modern farming: the arrival of mechanisation or, more accurately, of a new source of power. Strictly speaking, Marsh Farm is in the parish of Beaminster, but it lies much closer to the big house at Mapperton than either Coltleigh or Mapperton Farm, and much of it had been owned by the Brodrepps and Comptons since the late seventeenth

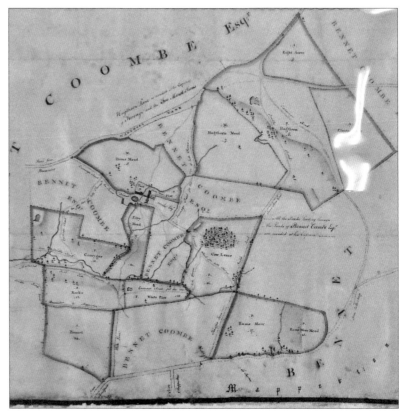

B. Pryce, Plan of Charity Lands in the parish of Beaminster 1776 – detail. [Dorset History Centre]

century. Ownership of the land had been divided between the Brodrepps and the trustees of Beaminster School that Frances Tucker had hoped to found. In 1871 Marsh Farm had extended over 420 acres with, in 1891, a population of thirty-seven people in five dwellings.

At the break-up of the estate in 1919, Marsh Farm was purchased by Bernard Cox (b.1863) the sitting tenant, who had previously had tenancies at South Poorton and Toller Whelme. He clearly set a standard of excellence in the presentation of stock, taking 'every fat stock prize except one at the Bridport Christmas fair'. Cox was succeeded by his son Ralph (1896-1980) in the hard years of the 1930s, a depression only ended by the sudden leap in demand caused by World War II. In March 1941 young Dick Berry arrived from blitzed London to be welcomed by the Cox family; 'they treated me as a son and with the farming staff soon knocked me into a farmer's boy'. The farm was still a substantial community. Milking of the sixty cows was done by hand; the two-furrow plough was handled by 'old Frank [Larcombe], the carter, with three horses'. Grass seed was 'sown by hand, or with a fiddle'. 'Harvesting and hay making and hoeing the root crops was a team effort'. 'If there was any job to be done on the farm it was done by hand, eight of us … topping hedges in the fall, digging banks, making hedges in the winter and the draining, always the draining'. What manual power could not achieve, the four horses and Kitty the old cob, essential at hay making, existed to do. Any other power source was occasional, like the old steam engine used for threshing.

> 'The old engine would pull into the rickyard, barrels would have to be filled with water the night before, coal to be hauled and ricks stripped of their thatch. Smoke and steam everywhere and rats to be knocked down as they escaped, but it was all very enjoyable and a real team job.'.

Otherwise 'sheep really took pride of place' at the farm, though Dick Berry was not at all interested in them. Previously Bernard Cox used to walk the lambs to the September sales in Dorchester, taking two or three days. Now the sheep were managed by Frank Larcombe's son Phil who was 'skilled in many farming crafts. With today's education advantages he would have gone far…'. It is a telling detail that the farmer's sons could afford to pay for their education at Beaminster Grammar School, while the children of his farm workers like Phil Larcombe, could not.

Dick Berry's time at Marsh Farm, 1941-1952, saw the beginning of mechanisation. There had been static machines there before, of course, but the new arrival was transformative. First came a standard Fordson tractor, costing £103 and a three furrow Ransome plough which cost over £40.

> 'I was put in charge of this new bit of machinery and it was the pride of my life. No

one on the farm had much idea how to use it so it was a sort of trial and error but in the end it did most of the heavy work, when we could get it started!'

Then a milking machine arrived. 'Where six of us used to milk, now one or two could manage'. And so farmworkers drifted elsewhere in search of work. In time their cottages would be bought up (or rented) by 'townspeople. Gone are the open fireplaces, the oil lamps and tin baths in front of the fire and the draughty loo at the end of the garden path.'

As early as the 1950s George Ewart Evans wrote in *Ask the Fellows who cut the Hay*: 'During the past fifty years or so the life of the countryside has been revolutionized and the rate of change within this period has been greater than it has ever been in recorded history'. The dissolution of the rural community implied by Dick Berry may have taken place a little later in the pastures of West Dorset than in the cornfields of Suffolk, but change was as abrupt, and as total.

Mythe

Neither of the other principal settlements in Mapperton can be documented with the depth or relative continuity of Coltleigh. Mapperton itself now consists of little more than the big house and the Rectory for the cottages that once clustered around them disappeared in the years after the plague. The transformation of Mythe is more total. Now all that remains is the tall gable end of a nondescript cottage, and behind it a lower wall encloses a room space open to the jackdaws. And it stands in rough woodland. During the centuries when Mythe was inhabited trees and any fallen timber would have been a vital resource for the inhabitants, but now the utter change in land usage over the past seventy years has allowed small trees to grow unhindered to provide cover for pheasants. The last house was largely demolished in the 1990s to provide building material and 200 tons of stone reused on a house up at Coltleigh. Of the stone taken up there, George Brown, who lived in it, remembered that only a wheelbarrow-full was left over.

Mythe, gable of ruined house.

In Anglo-Saxon, Mythe means the confluence of two streams. The importance of the settlement originally depended on its location: it was the site of a mill, indicated with unreal tidiness on the Tithe Map of 1841 by which time the land around it was absorbed into the principal tenancy at Mapperton Farm. Whether a mill was then still functioning must be doubtful.

Old photograph of house at Mythe.

In Domesday Book the mill at Mapperton had been worth 5s., compared to Castle Mill at Powerstock worth 3s., or the great mill at Cerne Abbas that ground corn for the abbey, worth 20s. Although the landscape will have much altered over the millennium, the actual fall of water can never have been great, nor very reliable. If, over the years 1590-1631 Richard Wiat, then his widow Alice and later millers were each presented to the Dean of Salisbury for profaning the sabbath by

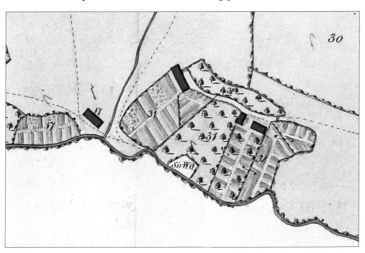

Tithe apportionment map, Mapperton, 1840 – detail: Mythe.
[Dorset History Centre]

running their mill, it is more likely they were taking advantage of useful rainfall in the valley than making a deliberate protest about Sunday observance. Tenants were however obliged to use the mill, and the manor court fined Hugh Munden for not doing so in 1606. The remains of a sluice close by where the mill house was placed in 1841 give some idea of this small scale operation – one of the last residents

Sluice on the stream at Mythe.

remembered washing her hair in water from the stream.

In 1590 the property had been described as consisting of 'a cottage with land called Bromy Close and another close called Waldich, a pasture called Longmead and a [water] mill called Meath Mill with two orchards'. These field names along with several others had disappeared by the time the Tithe Apportionment made 250 years later, except for 'Old Orchard' next door to the mill. In 1710 Robert Brodrepp bequeathed to his servant John Dorsett 'all that my Mill and Tenement… and all lands and closes thereto belonging' for 99 years. Dorsett seems to have sub-let the property for during the following decades the mill was occupied by the Barge family though how far milling continued into the eighteenth century is unknown.

Mythe was a comparatively large settlement. In 1841 eight houses were occupied, and their 35 occupants comprised more than a third of the inhabitants of the whole parish. It was not prosperous; heads of two of the four properties in 1861 were described as paupers, and among the employed, several were agricultural labourers. Gradually the number of houses occupied dwindled until before the first World War only one remained, lived in by the Legg family who had lived at Mythe in every previous census. David Legg was the estate woodman, living with his wife, five sons, and two others – one adopted and the other an elderly lady described in the official language of the time as 'imbecile'. It was their son John, 'Woodman's Labourer' aged fourteen at the time of the census, who was the only Mapperton man to die in World War 1. He and 1025 of the rest of the crew of HMS Invincible died when their ship was blown up and sank in ninety seconds at the battle of Jutland in May 1916. As a Stoker 1st. Class, and working in the torrid bowels of the ship, he will have known almost nothing of the great engagement on the surface above him.

After the War at least two cottages were occupied. Florrie Stephenson's memoir recalls details of growing up in a succession of cottages in and around Mythe in the late 1920s: cottages 'running alive with rats' and water needing to be fetched 150 yards along muddy paths. After living at Poorton with an open hearth fireplace up which you could see the stars and with 'a cauldron hanging, stewing something or boiling water', a cottage at Mythe seemed a 'really upmarket property'. The family was desperately poor: 'I can never remember having a whole egg; it was always cut in half'. Even so, climbing trees, bird-nesting and eating all the wild fruits, 'we had a wonderfully free life' interrupted only by school. The last residents seem to have been a family called Morgan in the 1940s, whose daughter walked up to the road beyond the rectory to catch the bus to school.

Mapperton Farm

From at least the mid-eighteenth century the bulk of the parish of Mapperton was treated as a single farm, probably based on the buildings still known as Mapperton Farm on the south-western edge of the parish. When records concerning it first become available in 1781 the tenant was Robert Conway, almost certainly a member of the prosperous clan that had lived at Lynch Farm in West Milton and Netherbury for more than a century. A decade earlier Mapperton had had the good fortune to be visited by the workaholic agricultural reformer, Arthur Young. His *Tours* through England, written in his late twenties established his reputation as an assiduous traveller, as a fount of information and as an agricultural reformer. He was in the habit of advertising his journeys in newspapers in advance and called upon

Mapperton Farm, view from west.

farmers who were interested to contact him, and accounts of his visits to their estates form the basis of his Tours. The account of his visit to Dorset forms much of the third volume of his misleadingly entitled *Farmer's Tour through the East of England* (1771), concentrating mostly on the central part of the county, particularly the great Damer estates based on Milton Abbas, and at Came. Mapperton was almost a wasted journey:

> 'From Bridport I went to Mapperton. Had Mr Broadrep been at home (to whom I had an introduction) I should have been able to have given a more particular account of the husbandry of the neighbourhood; but the following particulars were supplied by his tenant.'

It would be interesting to know whether Brodrepp had contacted Young in advance, or whether the latter was acting on some verbal recommendation picked up on his travels; both at least suggest Richard Brodrepp IV's active involvement in his estate. The account that the tenant, probably Conway, supplied was distilled by Young into a brief discussion of the rotation of crops, the cultivation of flax and hemp – said to be favoured 'chiefly for cleaning the land, for its great power for killing weeds' and the economics of sheep production. It was at this point that he observed that 'They depend much on lime for manuring'; Mapperton Farm has the remains of several kilns, including a fine example on Mythe Hill. Young was an

Limekiln, Mythe Hill.

ardent advocate of reforming practice, of the need to enclose and improve waste land and particularly the usefulness of turnips, as was being frequently practised in Norfolk. Dorset farmers were however sadly behind the times. At Mapperton Young confined himself to the briefest comment 'Nor are their turnips hoed', but the full force of this remark becomes apparent a few pages later, by which time he had got over into Somerset and at last fallen in with a like-minded farmer who had indeed come from Norfolk. This Mr. Cooper had worked for twenty years to introduce turnip cultivation, which resulted in his gaining 'infinitely more food than his neighbours'. Young goes on:

'Of these facts they [the neighbours] have now been regular witnesses near 20 years, and yet I could not find one man had imitated him'. It was a flagrant example 'of [their] stupidity and prejudice...It is intolerable; and a satire on the landlords for not exerting more spirit in a matter of such real importance.'

Gradually, however, improvement came. Thirty years later another visitor on his fact-finding mission for the Board of Agriculture spoke with Henry Legg, who had succeeded Robert Conway at Mapperton Farm, about several details of husbandry, his rotation of crops, the best moment for planting hemp and the management of sheep. Turnip cultivation and careful hoeing was now more widespread while potato growing had 'extended very rapidly' in gardens around Beaminster.

Young had enriched his agricultural journalism with detailed accounts of the principal country seats, such as Mr Frampton's 'new building' at Moreton and the 'magnificent new house' at Crichel. At Mapperton he was suddenly astonished by 'one of the most beautiful landscapes ever seen'. He was coming from Bridport to call at Mapperton Farm and, sitting on his horse, was raised a little above the deep lane and hedges on the way up from Melplash. The road skirts one of the many steeply sloping fields that drop towards the west. He caught sight of

'a small winding vale, so far beneath the point of view, that every field, hedge and tree, is distinctly commanded by one stroke of the eye. It is bounded on every side by cultivated hills; that on which you stand, [is] so steep a declivity, as to be perfectly 'romantic.'

Young had seen more landscape than most, and he knew what elements current aesthetic standards expected to be present in any view worthy of distinction. But this one was atypical. 'It is one of those most peculiar landscapes which, without water, strikes the imagination so forcibly, as to prevent your discovering the absence of it.' Authorities disagree on where this show-stopping view is. Some say it is to the east of the road, from the top of Mythe Hill beyond the sheep fold looking down towards Loscombe farm; others point in the other direction, west into the blue distance.

At the time of the Tithe Apportionment, Mapperton Farm had been in the hands of John Furmedge for perhaps thirty years. It was a considerable farm consisting of all the 350 best acres of Mapperton with another hundred in Netherbury and over sixty in Beaminster. At the break up of the estate in 1919 it was sold with 318 acres; the sale particulars singling out 'the old oak studded doors' of the farmhouse and the Famous Double Barn, 'the construction of its roof being a particularly good piece of workmanship'. Together with seven cottages and gardens this went to William Douch of Stourton Caundle for £3950. The MAF Farm Survey in June 1941 revealed mixed farming continuing; A.J.Douch had about 10% of his 340 acres under crops, while the rest was grazed by a herd of 124 sheep and 66 cattle, of which just under half were in milk. Nerissa Jones remembers Mr. Douch carrying milk up from the milking parlour with a wooden yoke. Since then the area and acreage of the farm has changed constantly: the present occupants farm 200 acres almost exclusively in Netherbury parish

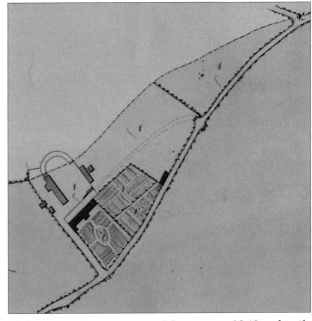

and perhaps they offer the view that so entranced Arthur Young to visitors to their exclusive, comfortably original and remote campsite.

The farmhouse has probably been rebuilt since the block plan shown on the Tithe Map, which, like the suggestion of a regular garden on the steep hill behind it, owes more to tidy-mindedness than to truth to the site. Only the west facing entrance may date back to the seventeenth century, and part of it was swept away in a landslip in 1953 which also put paid to the direct entrance shown in 1840.

To treat the Mapperton community

Tithe apportionment map, Mapperton, 1840 – detail: Mapperton Farm. [Dorset History Centre] only in terms of its constituent farms may exaggerate their separateness. It also focuses, perhaps unduly, on the principal tenants who show up in the records of the Manor Court, who appear as churchwardens and sidesmen and whose wills and inventories with their silver spoons, have survived. It ignores the mutual dependence of the community formed of undocumented daily contacts, the meetings at church and brief conversations, not to mention the physical contacts of homage and fealty. It overlooks the solicitude expressed in Richard Brodrepp I's will of 1656 where he names each of his principal tenants in 'Coltley and Meeth', giving them each a cloak for mourning and 'intreating them to live in unity and to attend gods ordinances conscionably', or 40s. left to 'old Thomas Knight' and £5 for placing the children of Cicely Turner in employment or apprenticeship.

The detailed accounts for the building of the new rectory, 1699-1703, provide an instance of the community at work and in relation to its immediate neighbourhood with unusual clarity. This was much the largest building operation in the village since the reconstruction of the big house forty years before. About sixty men, and John Legg's wife from Hooke, were involved at one time or another. The workforce brought together local men, specialist craftsmen from nearby villages but it was the constant stream of people fetching and carrying materials to the site that made the event exceptional. Much of the ordinary construction of the stone house was carried out by Thomas and Sam Gale who came up from Loscombe, just down the stream below Mythe. The Knight family of Mythe were also constantly employed from the moment they were 'drawing stones' from the little quarry in the rectory garden from which much of the stone was taken. Miscellaneous carpenter's work, sawing joists over the 'Great Parlour' and fixing doors was the work of Daniel Wade, churchwarden. John Munden, very likely the tenant at Coltleigh, made the twelve-mile journey over to Ham Hill to collect roof trusses. But it is the contacts between this local group and the stream of outsiders delivering materials that would have made the building campaign an unusual event. Farmers who happened to have timber would supply what they could: Brodrepp could offer 150 deal boards and his brother Dr. [Thomas] Brodrepp sold planks and timber and they were joined with Ruben Oliver from Evershot with elm boards, Mr Alford from Bridport with imported deal for floors, James Daw of Evershot with both oak and elm, and two others with oak. Thatching materials had to be sourced in the same way, so Messrs. Hallett from Wooth in Netherbury, Banger from Burcombe and Hain from Cattistock joined another group of suppliers of sheaves of reed. The bustle of these operations over the space of three years would have created common focus of interest and varied opportunities for meeting people, punctuated as it was by 'Ale given to the carters at Bargaining for Carriage', or 'a cheese for the masons' and '3 bushells of Malt to Brew Half an Hogshead of Ale for them'.

IV

All Saints Church

All Saints, Mapperton, interior view.

Little inside the present church gives an impression of great age. The seating is mostly Victorian pitch pine; the walls are painted and no memorial dates before the mid-eighteenth century. Only the twelfth century font, now standing beneath the tower, may reach back to an original stone building on this site. The chancel walls are, apparently, medieval but the nave was rebuilt in 1704. Like most English churches of whatever size, All Saints, Mapperton, is a palimpsest, its contents reflecting some of the changes in belief, liturgical custom and architectural style of the past thousand years.

As a separate parish Mapperton probably developed from the initiative of a local landowner in the period following the Norman invasion, but it functioned as a dependent chapel of Netherbury which, in the period before distinct parishes had become formalised, exercised authority over a wider area. Some chapels never gained authority for the full range of functions of christening and burial, and as far as burial at Mapperton was concerned this was to persist, not least because the rocky foundations of the churchyard made burial virtually impossible. Mary, the heiress of the Morgans, had a vault under the chancel 'hewn out of this rock of her inheritance' for her burial there in 1650, but apart from her family there are few other burials, and in their wills Mapperton people always spoke of burial at Netherbury.

The pace at which the religious changes of the Reformation made themselves felt in this corner of the King's realm is not clear. While several members of the community remained loyal to the old religion, changes in practice enjoined by the succession of royal

Injunctions do seem to have been complied with. The Injunctions of 1547 insisted that services should be conducted in English, and banned processions and with them, the repeated ringing of bells, 'except one bell … to be rung before the sermon'. In 1555 Mapperton still had two bells, but the redundant bell was disposed of soon after. This caused ill-feeling – for financial rather than religious reasons, for the church wardens stated that 'Mr Robert Morgan solde a bell of the churches for how much we know nott which cost at the first £7 of which John Roper John Trevytt layd out 26s.6d'. The present bell dates from the eighteenth century. Any fragments of the medieval fittings in the church that did not disappear in the 1550s would have been obliterated in the 1590s with the arrival of the combative puritan George Bowden, first as school master and then as minister at Mapperton. Until then there appears to have been little pressure for change and the few families that refused to attend the church probably masked a larger group of others who remained loyal to the old religion while finding little difficulty with outward conformity, at least to the extent of attending the church. The range and vehemence of Bowden's antagonism to everything from kneeling on entering the church to wearing a surplice suggests that a clean sweep was made of all internal decoration. Away went the paintings, images, lights, and possibly stained glass that had illuminated the medieval interior. Only a memory remained. In the later part of Elizabeth's reign, a villager recalled that 'we hadd a plott of grownde to maynteyne two toches [lights, placed before images] and whan the Englysshe s(er)vice was used the rent was stayed & so yt is yett'. At Wytherston there is a field called 'Lamp Ground' which no doubt had once served an identical purpose to the field remembered at Mapperton. The entire turmoil of the Reformation is here encapsulated as the moment when the 'Englysshe' service was introduced. The ways in which people remembered the changes wrought by the reformation in the decades that followed, as in Shakespeare's evocation of 'bare ruin'd choirs, where late the sweet birds sang' has recently been carefully studied. The Mapperton memory is apparently unique. No great monastery was in the immediate vicinity and no land at Mapperton had belonged to any religious house, so Reformation did not bring any sudden change of landownership, as was the case at Powerstock or West Milton and so many other places.

Bowden's puritan attitudes persisted in the religious leadership of the parish over a long period. For the next century to 1698 Mapperton had the service of just three rectors, each of which appears to have continued in Bowden's footsteps and the selection of such men reveals the doctrinal preferences of their patron. On Bowden's death in 1640 Richard Brodrepp I appointed Hugh Gundry, an Oxford graduate who had served previously at Wellington in Somerset, and it is his hand that writes the names in the first surviving Parish Register. The religious loyalties of the parish at this time are demonstrated by a special collection taken in May 1655. In the middle of the previous winter Europe was stunned at the fierce persecution by the Catholic Duke of Savoy of the ancient dissenting sect of Waldensians in the Alpine mountains. As many as 1700 were killed. Many more fled as Swiss and Dutch Protestants organised safe routes to guide them to safety. In England Milton wrote his great sonnet, 'Avenge O Lord thy slaughtered saints' to express his horror. Cromwell, enraged, exerted diplomatic pressure on France to bring the massacre to an end. In May a nationwide collection was organised, a huge version of the briefs by which parishes used to raise money for other parishes in distress from fire or local disaster. This was Cromwellian 'Live Aid'. A contemporary list provides the detailed evidence. £38,097.7s.3d was raised nationwide. Cromwell himself gave £2000, Edward Montagu £30. In that list Dorset, a smallish county with few towns of any size, raised the sixth highest total, £901, behind populous Essex or Norfolk and huge Yorkshire. Considering the population of this tiny parish, its contribution of £1.14s.0d. is impressive and compares with Loders at £2.16s.6d., or Powerstock's £3.11s.7d. No doubt the lord of the manor's contribution was helpful, but the parochial effort was a good deal more than they had contributed for the terrible fire that had devastated Marlborough two years before.

The Restoration of the monarchy saw the return of a triumphant Anglican church and the abandonment of any compromise with the religious innovations of the previous twenty years. By an Act of Uniformity of 1662 all those clergy who refused to accept the entire Prayer Book by St Bartholomew's Day (24 August) were to be ejected from their livings. Hugh Gundry was one such; he was later to be found preaching at a dissenting chapel near Aylesbeare in Devon. As the great nonconformist memorialist Edmund Calamy wrote of him,'he continu'd a Nonconformist all his Days; and liv'd and dy'd in a contented though no very splendid Condition.'

The presence of these ejected ministers throughout the countryside – they were forbidden to come within five miles of towns, and concentrated in some areas not least west Dorset, south Somerset and around Taunton – was an added ingredient of the febrile religious and political atmosphere in the decades after 1660, at a time when the royal government seemed both in foreign and domestic policies to be favouring Catholics.

Bernard Banger who replaced Gundry on his ejection in 1662 is likely to have been a son of a vicar of Frampton and brother of Josiah, the vicar of Broadhembury who had been imprisoned with other dissenters at Dorchester in 1663 and ejected from his living in 1666. But Josiah bounced back and by the 1690s he was living in Sherborne where he had a share in the meeting house and he lies under a chest tomb at Lillington with its unique acrostic inscription. His brother Bernard, who was perhaps not so financially independent, chose to accept the harsh conditions of conformity under the 'Clarendon Code'. There was one gesture of resistance in 1670, when it was reported that he had refused to wear the surplice for divine service, but he gave in, promising that 'hee…will in all things bee conformable to the discipline of the Church of England'. At least we may conclude that worship at Mapperton will not have diverged too far from the puritan – dissenting tradition set by his two predecessors. Banger served the community for thirty-five years and died in office. Apart from his '4 shelves and his Bookes' there's nothing in either his will or his inventory to distinguish him from other mildly prosperous inhabitants of west Dorset.

The eighteenth century clergy that succeeded these controversial figures in the Rectory of Mapperton have left little evidence of any great religious activity. John Powell's enduring monument is the Rectory but the parish register, conscientiously signed by him on each of its (few) pages between 1703 and 1734 at least suggests his presence here. Less can be said of John Marshall, Fellow of University College, Oxford, who held the living next for twenty years. His will deals with his property in Co. Durham, but the poor of Mapperton were to be remembered if he was still Rector there at the time of his death. With his successor Thomas Fox (c.1716-1793) instituted at Mapperton in 1757, the rector's signature reappears on the register and he was certainly a local figure. He was the son of Baruch Fox, a prosperous mercer and Master of the Sherborne Almshouse. During his long incumbency at Mapperton Thomas accumulated other livings including West Chelborough and Abbas Combe, six miles north-east of Sherborne, and it was his wish that at his funeral he should be 'carried to church

by six parish Clerks two from Chelborow the old and New one from Combe one from Allington One from Mapperton One from Glanville Wootton'. It is not easy to estimate the combined income from these livings, but a comfortable life was assured. Mapperton itself, with its modern Rectory was not a poor living, and Fox clearly used his inherited wealth intended, as his father's will had stated, 'for [his] better setting up in business' to good effect. His son, Thomas jnr. (1747-1820) served as his father's curate at Mapperton and had the Rectory at Wootton Glanville ready for him on leaving Oxford in 1770. He is the only figure of Mapperton's more distant history of whom a likeness survives. A portrait of him as an

Attrib. Thomas Beach, Portrait of Thomas Fox jnr., early 1760s.

adolescent survives in the possession of his descendants, painted perhaps in the early 1760s and is most likely the work of Reynolds's pupil, Thomas Beach. An inscription, written in 1841 by the sitter's son, then himself Rector of Mapperton records: 'This Portrait supposed to be an early Work of Sir Joshua Reynolds was painted at the request of Richard Brodrepp Esq. of Mapperton, who presented the boy with a cocked hat for the occasion'.

Succession to the Rectory at Mapperton was not a foregone conclusion however, for in a rather formal letter of 1778 Bennet Combe, heir to Richard Brodrepp IV, wrote that he did 'not chose to make any Promise at present with regard to the next Presentation to the Parsonage'. Three years later however, his tone had entirely changed and he wrote another of his idiosyncratic letters, with its text crammed up into an upper corner of the sheet:

> 'In Case it shall be at the Death of your Father be agreeable to you to succeed him in the Parsonage of Maperton, I shall be happy to present you to it. I am with the greatest Regard, My Dear Tom, Your real Friend, Bennet Combe.'

Thomas did not have to wait for the death of his father to succeed to Mapperton, but he does not seem to have chosen to live here. He began to build the new Rectory at Wootton Glanville, and the Mapperton Rectory was often advertised to let in the 1790s.

With the inheritance of Mapperton by the Comptons of Minstead, the Rectory was used as an additional income stream for clerical members of the family. When Thomas Fox jnr. died in 1820, Henry Combe Compton appointed his younger brother John to the post and, while on his death in 1835 Thomas Fox's son Charles was able to secure the succession, he had to agree to resign if either of Compton's sons should chose to hold the living. And indeed he resigned in 1848 so that a third son, Paulet Mildmay Compton, could succeed to a living he then held for fifty-eight years.

The curates who carried out the weekly services are much less fully remembered, nor is there any record of members of the Mapperton congregation who, following the independent traditions of their seventeenth-century forbears, absented themselves from this conventional worldliness and slipped down to the meeting house in Beaminster, or went to hear John Wesley preach.

The Rectory and its Glebe

Banger, Gundry, Bowden and Peter Beauchamp before them lived in a vanished rectory whose site is not known. It was replaced by the present Old Rectory in 1704. The earliest description of a previous rectory dates from 1405, when it was described as 'built with one hall, with chambers on either side, one barn, one cowhouse and one kitchen, which have suffered decay in the timber-work and walls by default of the rector'. In 1628

Mapperton Rectory.

the area round the rectory is described a little more fully as containing a 'Barne & two out houses belonging to the same. One little Medow & two garden plots one Orchard one Court thereunto belonginge contayning in all by estimacon one acre & halfe'. Eighty years later this building was pulled down and an entirely new rectory was erected soon after his arrival by Revd.

Rectory doorway, initials of Revd. John Powell.

John Powell who had his initials carved at his going out and coming in. This building has the distinction of being one of Dorset's best documented building operations for which records survive and its workforce is discussed in Part III. The building has changed little; originally the southern half of the ground floor was divided into two rooms and the roof was thatched at least until 1848 when the Revd. Paulet Mildmay Compton began his long incumbency. In about 1880 he moved to the big house and the rectory was let. The porch proclaims that it was 'restored' by the rector in 1890. Perhaps that was when tiles replaced thatch.

Rectory doorway, Revd. Paulet Compton's inscription.

The rectory was for much of this period a working farmstead from which successive incumbents farmed their *glebe*, the land belonging to the church from which a significant part of their income was derived. Mapperton's glebe was at 56 acres extensive for the tiny size of the parish; Powerstock's was 76 out of over 3,000 acres, Hooke's 32. The inventory of Bernard Banger, rector from 1662 to 1698, shows some details of this self-sufficiency, for he was appraised at 'Six Milch Cows Two Bulls one heifer'. The rectory had a Brewhouse, containing a 'Brewing Tubb, three other Tubbs one Cheese [stone] One Churne', and in the Buttery there were four half-hogsheads among what was termed 'the rest of the lumber'. Another item, lumped with 'things forgotten' were 'Bees'. The relatively extensive glebe was no doubt largely leased to local tenants, as it was to Roger Knight in 1603. Its fields were located in different parts of the parish, but by 1840 the glebe was concentrated into two substantial areas of thirty-six and twelve acres south and south west of the big house. It had not always been thus. The early seventeenth century terriers [detailed lists of landholdings] give only loose locations of the principal glebe fields with names forgotten by the time the Tithe Apportionment recorded them in 1840, but one is 'a plot of Meadow grownd conteyning one acre or ther about lying at Colt wood'. That the Rector did have land on Coltleigh hill is borne out by some chance entries in the Parish Register in 1801: 'The trees in Coltley hill Brow above Cuniger Mead [more often 'Coniger', a rabbit warren] planted 1765. One hundred and eighty Elm Trees were planted on Bushy Close & Five Acres by Thos Fox Rector'. To which is added a note 'Cut down 1835. They were nearly all Scotch Fir. The Brow was replanted with Firs and Forest Trees 1837. Charles Fox Rector'.

To the profits of farming the glebe, which clearly included the long-term profits from timber whether directly or through a lease, should be added the income from tithes. This tenth part payment on all agricultural produce also varied greatly between parishes: at Hooke the vicar could count on only £16, at Powerstock £105; at Mapperton the income from Tithe was £30. In all, the rector of Mapperton enjoyed an income of £61.10s. at a time when a skilled master mason might be paid twelve or fourteen pence a day, with perhaps an extra two or three pence allowance for food, or perhaps £17 in a year – if employment were continuous. Both clergy and artisan would supplement that income from a smallholding or, in the clergy case, from the glebe.

The present Church

In 1704 Richard Brodrepp II rebuilt the nave of his parish church making no concessions, for example in the matter of the design of windows, to any changes in architectural taste that might be associated with the Age of Wren: their design is close to the windows on the fraternity chapel at Stalbridge, built in the early sixteenth century. This was of course a deliberate choice. Many years earlier Brodrepp had installed windows of a much more

All Saints, Mapperton, exterior view of nave.

'modern' design in the main house and, to a different design, at the stables. But this, gothic survival rather than Gothic Revival, was seen as an appropriate form for churches. At the same time, the Revd. John Powell attended to the chancel; it may have been reroofed at this time and its floor was tiled with 300 'potters tiles'. Perhaps this was when the east window was blocked up and covered with some wooden reredos, to be opened up again in 1845-6.

After that there is silence concerning the church for over seventy years. Unfortunately this covers two significant alterations to the building. A laconic note in the Parish Register states that the tower was taken down in 1766. It is said to have dated from the fifteenth century and Hutchins, whose visit to the house must have been before this, described it as embattled and pinnacled. Some similarly tiny local churches like Wraxall and Frome Vauchurch never had towers; Lillington got one, courtesy of a bequest, in about 1529. Perhaps the original tower at Mapperton had been the result of generosity from the Morgans.

The other significant alteration was the introduction of stained glass in the nave. The church has two distinct series of stained glass panels. One, a group of armorial roundels of early sixteenth century origin, stand at the top of the lights on each north and south window. The other series are small designs set, often within circular or square borders, lower down in the same lights. Thirty-two of these are of continental origin and have been associated with several centres in the Low countries and France. They can be associated with a scrap torn from an account book of Richard Brodrepp IV which records, for April 1768 'Painted glass for the church £10.10s.'. A fashion for buying imported stained glass was developing at this time, led by influential collectors such as Horace Walpole, decorating his house at Strawberry Hill.

From 1774 churchwarden's accounts give some idea of the year-by-year costs for repairs, generally for reglazing or repairs to the roof. There must have been a severe storm in

1781 that called for 'half a hund[redweight] of Read to cover the church after the high wind 9s.', then to William Hallett 'for twigs and laying it up', followed by £3.11s.6d to William Mills for 'retiling the Church'.

By the 1840s enthusiasm for church restoration was widespread. Robert Williams at Bridehead had been the driving force in the restoration of the churches at Compton Valance and All Saints, Dorchester (1843), while Bradpole church was much extended in 1844. Locally, the most important new building was the entirely new parish church and school at Melplash in 1845, the consecration of which was attended by 4,000 people with cannon firing and a procession in which the master mason carried a silver trowel and thirty or forty of the neighbouring clergy wore academical dress. The initiative to do something at Mapperton may have come from Capt. Richard Atchison R.N., then tenant of the house and Henry Compton's son-in-law. In 1845 he became churchwarden and two guineas was paid for an 'estimate for necessary repairs to the church' from Richard Warr of Beaminster. Warr advertised himself as 'Auctioneer, Surveyor, Undertaker' and the first of these professions was much the most active. As surveyor he appears to have been in charge of repairs at Swyre church in 1846, and was later to build the church at Toller Whelme. In an age of increasing sophistication in church architecture – Benjamin Ferrey's use of the briefly fashionable neo-Norman style at Melplash is an example – Warr was no doubt a competent builder but with few pretensions to 'art'.

Initial worries about the state of the roof led to a more thorough overhaul. The principal tenant farmers agreed a rate of three shillings in the pound to pay for repairs, but in the event much of the interior work was paid for by 'private funds', so that the parish had only to meet the cost of a new roof most of which was constructed by Joseph Gibbs of Bradpole. A note in the churchwarden's accounts summarises what was achieved:

All Saints, Mapperton, west window.

> 'The Church was entirely gutted, the Gallery taken down, the East window restored, which was built up, the south window in the Chancel was built up, and a door knocked out into a room of the Mansion, the west window was repaired, the church repewed and the whole put into thorough and substantial repair'.

The glass for the newly-liberated east window was given by Mrs. Compton and in 1851 her son-in-law, Capt. Atchison commissioned the west window in memory of his son from O'Connor of Berners St.

*All Saints, Mapperton,
font, C12th.*

*All Saints, Mapperton, photograph showing earlier
position of font.*

The font now in the church is, as in many churches, the oldest element in the building. It appears to have been rediscovered in an outhouse in the 1840s and an old photograph shows it standing beneath the chancel arch from where it has been moved to the west end. Mapperton's bowl is Norman, and similar to that at Whitestaunton beyond Chard; the base is modern.

*St. Andrew, Whitestaunton,
Somerset. Font, C12th.*

The twentieth century saw many changes in the official and administrative status of the church at Mapperton. A vestry was added in 1908, and several memorials have been erected starting with the reliefs in memory of Charles Labouchère on either side of the east window by the distinguished medallist and sculptor Cecil Thomas. In 1919 Mrs. Labouchère had purchased the advowson for £1000, and in the following year she bought the glebe lands. She inherited Revd. Charles Earle as her Rector who had been appointed in 1907; following his death during World War II no successor was appointed, and the parish was later joined with

*C. Thomas, Relief in memory of
Charles Labouchère, 1926.*

Melplash. When the church was declared redundant in 1977 Victor Montagu purchased the building from the diocese although some fittings initially stayed with Salisbury. Eventually the need for continued maintenance allowed the family to take over entire ownership of the building and its contents, and careful attention to its needs continues. The church has been used for regular services in each year, besides concerts.

A note on the stained glass

The stained glass at Mapperton consists principally of sixty-one small panels, mostly roundels or rectangular, set in the opaque glass of the six nave windows. They have been much commented upon, but their provenance and present arrangement are by no means clear. Apart from a dozen panels that are either assemblages of fragments, incomplete or indecipherable, they divide into two main types.

At the top of each light are placed eight single roundels of early sixteenth-century English origin, the main examples of a group of twenty. The top panels are enclosed by borders, four of which contain the Garter motto; the others are floral.

The second set form a group of thirty two panels of continental origin. These have been inventoried by the *Corpus Vitrearum Medii Aevi*, which locates their manufacture in the Low countries and France. A few depicting particular scenes from scripture are linked to the style of Jan Swart, active in Antwerp of *c.* 1525. One of the earliest, dated 1509, is thought to be French. Others are purely decorative of *c.*1540. These continental panels can be associated with the scrap torn from an account book of Richard Brodrepp IV recording, for April 1768 'Painted glass for the church £10.10s.'. Brodrepp was in London knowing where he would be able to purchase the newly fashionable continental glass from one of the dealers supplying antiquarian collectors such as Horace Walpole. Two other panels consist of fragments of the same origin, but broken and rearranged since their arrival here.

All Saints, Mapperton, stained glass: Visitation, manner of Jan Swart.	*All Saints, Mapperton, stained glass: head, dated 1509.*	*All Saints, Mapperton, stained glass: putto.*	*All Saints, Mapperton, stained glass: wild man.*

Engraving of stained glass commemorating Trenchard –Morgan marriage, early C17th. formerly at Wolfeton House.

Roundels of armorial glass were a common decoration in secular halls in the early sixteenth century England. Hutchins published engravings of similar glass at Wolfeton and described the collections at Milton Abbey, Bingham's Melcombe and Parnham. Most of the families represented in these cases were connections by marriage; early collections also included local monastic houses, and many included prominent local families linked by considerations of patronage. An account of Mapperton's armorial roundels is complicated by the different accounts given for their origin. Hutchins said nothing about them in 1774, but he did mention a list of *c*.1600 of the armorial glass then in the old hall. In the third edition of Hutchins of 1863, the editors added that Mr Brodrepp had used glass from Parnham in his church; and a later account of 1914 added that Brodrepp had also taken glass from Beaminster church and Lower Meerhay. If the installation of the roundels really was the work of Brodrepp, then it must have taken place before the end of that family in 1774. In 1913 *Country Life* offered a new explanation, that the glass was 'found in a box at Mapperton by Capt. Robert Atchison, son in law of Henry Combe Compton and placed in the church during the restoration of the middle of the nineteenth century'. This circumstantial account appears reliable, but Hutchins's list of the armorial glass in the church of 1863 does not describe what is there now, though continuing wear, breakage, rearrangement and corrosion have left some panels in very poor condition. The arms of Peverell, of Bradford Peverell until the reign of Henry VIII, occur twice, but there is no known connection with this family. By contrast, neither of the arms of Christopher Morgan's wives, Marie Brett of Whitestaunton (d.1582) and Ann Bampfyld of Poltimore are present (though both alliances are referenced in the home churches of the wives). This supports the idea of an origin for the glass before 1580. The collection of armorial glass is more miscellaneous and confused than accounts have allowed although at least one roundel, clearly from the hall at Mapperton [page 71] shows the intense awareness of his ancestry that characterises Robert Morgan's building.

Glass in the east and west windows form part of the restoration of the church in 1845. The east window of *c*.1846 was given by Mrs Compton and designed by her sister-in-law, Mrs Selina Bracebridge, an artist who had been a pupil of Samuel Prout, but better known as an early and active supporter of Florence Nightingale. The west window followed in 1850, given by Mrs Compton's son-in-law, Capt. Aitchison in memory of his son William. It was designed by M.O'Connor of Berners St., and installed by John Trask, probably the Yeovil glazier of that name.

All Saints, Mapperton, stained glass panel, formerly in Hall.

Analysis of heraldry of roundel in north-west window of nave, provided by College of Arms

1. *Argent on a Bend Sable a Fleur de lis two Cinquefoils Argent on a Chief flory between two Lees Or.* A more complicated version of the arms awarded to John **Morgan** in 1528. The chief is not always present.

2. *Or a Lion in a bordure engrailed vert.* **Muckleston**. Mary, daughter and coheir of John Muckleston of Staffordshire married John Bryte, and their daughter and heiress married John Morgan.

3. *Azure on a Fess between three Crescents Or.* **Brett or Bryt** of Mapperton. These should precede Muckleston. [Not to be confused with Brett of Whitestaunton.]

4. *Or a Lion rampant Gules.* **Legh of Staffordshire**. The link appears to be through Margaret (not Mary as in 2, above) daughter of John Muckleston, son and heir of Adam Muckleston son and heir of another Adam Muckleston and his wife Ceycelle daughter and one of the heirs of Reginald Legh of Legh, Staffs.

This coat, which appears in other panels, impales a coat of six quarters.

1 **Aston of Tixall**. John Morgan married Ellen, daughter of Sir John Aston of Tixall, Staffs.

2. perhaps Littleton; 3. unidentified; 4. ?Staunton; 5. possibly Byron; 6 Unidentified.

V

'To Lett'

So with the house empty and the doors locked and the mattresses rolled round, those
stray airs, advance guards of great armies, blustered in, brushed bare boards, nibbled
and fanned, met nothing in bedroom or drawing-room that wholly resisted them but
only hangings that flapped, wood that creaked, the bare legs of tables, saucepans and
china already furred, tarnished, cracked. What people had left and shed – a pair of
shoes, a shooting cap, some faded skirts and coats in wardrobes – these alone kept the
human shape and the emptiness indicated how once they were filled and animated…

Virginia Woolf

From about 1775 the house and fields of Mapperton became an outlier to the estate of
the Compton family of Minstead in the New Forest. The house was let to an irregular
succession of tenants but for the first forty years nothing seems to be known of the house
at all. Virginia Woolf's vivid picture of Talland House in *To the Lighthouse* (1927) left
unvisited by its summer tenants during the first World War captures that unwitnessed life. No
doubt Mapperton wasn't always empty, but gradually its contents would have been depleted,
whether to Minstead, deliberately, or by others taking advantage.

From 1828 tenants are noticed. For about six years from that date the house was taken
by Sir Molyneux Hyde Nepean, who had inherited Loders Court on the death of his father, the
Secretary for Ireland and sometime governor of Bombay. When he left there was a substantial
house sale at Mapperton, but the items sold – the '120-piece Angouleme china dinner service,
mahogany cabinet piano forte, 70 doz. of wines and 800 volumes of books' seem to have
come from Loders. By 1841 the house was lived in by the wealthy young High Churchman,
William Maskell, briefly vicar of Corscombe, who witnessed the inquest following a murder
at Nettlecombe in 1839 and was deeply shocked to see the arsenic-ridden bodies dissected on
the communion table in Powerstock church. Later tenants were military men on leave. One
of them, a relative of the Comptons, Capt. Aitchison, took an active part in the restoration
of the church in 1845-6. His successor, a retired Lieutenant Colonel Marryatt, stayed for a
decade from 1859 and saw the marriages of two daughters into local families. After that,
another solution for the empty house was for H. C. Compton's uncle the rector to take over

the house, which he did for the last twenty-five years of his life from about 1881.

The Revd. Paulet Mildmay Compton (1823-1906), for almost sixty years Rector, with the additional sinecure of Wytherston, should be a dominant personality in an account of Victorian Mapperton. He was a wealthy man, he enjoyed fox hunting, he can be seen attending all the small local meetings and assemblies that he should have attended, and local friends were made in clerical circles one of whom, Canon William Gildea of Netherbury, gave what was probably the first public lecture on the house. He was married and had one daughter. His wife Mary was vice-president of the local branch of the Primrose League. Compton can be seen, through the deferential eyes of the *Dorset County Chronicle*, celebrating the marriage of the Prince of Wales in March 1863.

'All labourers were granted a half day by their employers and the families were bountifully supplied with the means of feasting by the Rector and his friends'.

It was not a perfect day. Snow lay on the ground in the morning, which the newspaper courteously interpreted as 'an emblem of the spotless purity of the bride'. Festivities were intended for the evening, when:

'in spite of the rain which had fallen steadily since noon, the labourers and their families collected outside the old Manor House soon after dark. They all wore wedding favours and their happy remarks showed how thoroughly they enjoyed the occasion, and how little they cared for the damping effects of the rain, which, as if in approbation of their loyalty, ceased for a time. When they had assembled their pastor addressed them. He pointed out the blessings enjoyed by all classes of Englishmen under the monarchy as now established; he expressed the wish of all present that the marriage of that day might result in great happiness as well to the nation as to the royal pair and then called upon them to give three hearty cheers for the Prince and Princess of Wales. The clergyman waved his hat, and was about to lead the cheering, when, with a fervour that could not be equalled, his flock uttered a loud "A-a-armen"; a very appropriate conclusion they no doubt considered to his address, but one which was very ludicrous.'

All were supplied with torches which lit up 'the Elizabethan gables, the old windows of the house…the old English court-yard outside, and, beyond all the faces of the loyal and happy company.' After that everybody went up the hill to Coltleigh, where a rain-sodden bonfire was eventually lit and answered by five others on the surrounding hills. Twenty one rockets, specially obtained from London, were set off, the National Anthem sung and some verses spoken, but although the rain 'soon compelled the ladies to retire, the proceedings closed with three times three cheers for the Prince and Princess of Wales.'

Paulet Compton will have been responsible for the establishment of a village school. There is little evidence of such an institution in the village at any time since the 1590s, when the churchwardens complained, rather unfairly, that George Bowden's holding a school in the church meant that it became 'disordered'. Later rectors may also have included an

Mapperton, school.

element of reading and perhaps writing in their Sunday school. The existing building is said to have been constructed in 1880 but Compton had advertised for a 'Dame Schoolmistress' a dozen years earlier, offering a good house and garden, and by 1875 Miss Sarah Barrett was in post. A Log Book survives for twenty years from 1877 in which attendance rose from thirteen to forty. The Rector's family, and particularly his daughter Alice, were constantly popping in, to choose a place for the new map, to bring new books for reading or to listen to 'intelligent answers' to Scripture. The demands of farming ensured children's absence for the hay harvest or for gleaning, but there were also days off for the Beaminster Fair, for the Cattle Fair and 'a holiday on account of the Primrose (League) Fete'. The school ceased sometime in the 1920s.

Sometime before 1881 Compton moved from the Rectory to the main house. His daughter Alice was now adult and had taken on managing livestock, which she advertised for sale through the local paper. It was at the manor house that Compton gave a dinner to celebrate the Queen's Jubilee, the event brought forward because he was going abroad. Over sixty sat down to enjoy the cooking of Mrs Lord the housekeeper, followed by humorous speeches. Then 'dancing was indulged in till late, the proceedings being characterised with that delightful informality which makes these Arcadian gatherings so enjoyable'. Another celebration, as described by the deeply conservative *Dorset County Chronicle*, caught the occasion of the coming of age visit of the young heir, Henry Francis Compton, in February 1893. 'He was met by his woodmen and the employees of his uncle, … the horses were taken from the carriage, and he was drawn to his ancestral mansion'. In the afternoon Compton gave a school treat. The schoolroom was decked with flags, a 'most liberal' tea provided and a 'very interesting magic lantern entertainment' took place with an instructive lecture, followed by a speech thanking the young squire. 'God Save the Queen' was sung. Inside the enclosed 'Arcadian' vision of the ancestral estate at Mapperton as portrayed by newspapers the stable world of deference and loyalty might seem everlasting. Viewed from further away, the long agricultural depression rendered its continuance far from certain.

The Long Twentieth Century

One result of the long period during which Mapperton was occupied by tenants was that the building remained unaltered. No handsome modern neo-Gothic country seat replaced its dated charm. With the bulk of the land being farmed from Mapperton Farm on the south-west edge of the parish, the house was unlikely to degenerate into a working farmhouse only to be rescued in the twentieth century by an injection of wealth from a source other than land.

After his uncle Paulet Compton died early in 1906 aged eighty-three the young head of the family, Henry Francis Compton (1872-1943), turned his attention to the Dorset estate to which he had been introduced so glowingly on his coming-of-age twelve years earlier. In fact attention to his Dorset estate provided a needful diversion. He had recently endured a traumatic three months, in which he had stood for Parliament in a Hampshire by-election and been, just, elected while the government he supported resigned just two days before his poll. In the ensuing General Election the Conservatives were defeated by the resurgent Liberals with Compton one of its many casualties so that he never took his seat. He had been an elected MP for a matter of days.

Compton's Dorset estate included two substantial houses in Mapperton and Melplash besides land estimated in 1883 to extend just over 3,000 acres. Using the rough figures of acreage and income provided by Bateman's *Great Landowners of Great Britain*, the ten greatest landowners in the eastern, corn-growing, side of the county (Pitt-Rivers, Wingfield Digby, Bankes, Lord Wimborne etc.) managed to make £1 per acre from their extensive estates, but the average for the ten biggest estates in the west of the county (including Ilchester, Weld, Erle Drax [then at Holnest], the Duke of Bedford [Swire, Long Bredy] and which included, at No. 25, Henry Compton) the return was over 10% less. The later nineteenth century decline in agricultural prices, caused by intense foreign competition in grain from the American prairies or from refrigerated meat from the Argentine and Australia, damaged English farming irrevocably and estates in west Dorset had little defence. The prospect was not encouraging. The next-door estate based on Hooke, which included most of Powerstock and belonged to the Earls of Sandwich, then of Hinchingbrooke, Hunts. [with 5286 acres in Dorset], faced the same predicament. It was about to be lotted up and sold.

Compton's attention focussed initially on buildings. He helped pay for the building of the vestry to the church in 1908 and a new gamekeeper's cottage was built in 1910. In the main house a new water supply, gas lighting and suites of bathrooms were installed. Much more interestingly, he brought in the Jacobean chimneypieces to the big house, denuding Melplash in the process. This was only the most visible part of his deliberate restoration of the house to a particular period of its past, other aspects of which can only be known indirectly. When *Country Life* devoted an article to the house in October 1913 it noted that the 'remaining windows [of the north wing] have lately been restored to correspond with' the 'mullion windows with arched heads on the western face and the south gable' which 'are original'. This discrimination between what were taken to be original windows of c1550 and other windows was indebted to an account of the house published by Canon

Chimney piece formerly at Melplash Court, now in the Hall, Mapperton.

Gildea of Netherbury in 1899, after having been delivered to a visiting party from the Dorset Field Club. Another detail of the restoration of the interior was recorded by Richard Hine the historian of Beaminster, who mentioned that the early renaissance overmantel with the Morgan arms in the room over the Drawing Room 'was discovered beneath the oak panelling when the house underwent a restoration on the death of Rev. Paulet Mildmay Compton in 1906'. Whether Henry Compton had plans to install a 'period' ceiling in the hall, as Mrs. Labouchère was to do after the war, remains unknown, as does the name of his advisor.

On its earliest visit to Mapperton in 1901 *Country Life* had talked of its 'true old

Binghams Melcombe, from J Nash, Mansions of the Olden Time, 1840.

English domestic picturesqueness', reprising the vision of a place untouched by the modern world evoked in newspaper reports of Henry Compton's coming of age and before that of the celebration of the wedding of the Prince of Wales. Nostalgia for uniquely English, Jacobethan architecture was a mood of the times, although it had been stimulated much earlier by the romantic illustrations of Joseph Nash's *Mansions of England in the Olden Time* (1839-49) that had offered vivid recreations of houses of the age of Henry VIII and Good Queen Bess, some set in Dorset houses such as Athelhampton, Waterston and Binghams Melcombe. Neighbouring houses were undergoing similar restoration. The restoration of Athelhampton after its sale in 1891 has recently been described as 'at the vanguard of an important shift in the aesthetic mood of late Victorian England'. The last heir of the Oglanders had sold Parnham in 1896, and a more thorough-going redecoration began there, aided by the import of a varied range of foreign materials, not least Italian choir stalls for the dining room. At Montacute the neglected and impoverished house of the Phelips family had seen the beginnings of restoration in the re-erection of the entrance front from Clifton Maybank – itself a contemporary to Mapperton – in 1786, and the process was continued when Lord Curzon rented the house from 1916 and bought in panelling and ceilings available on the London market. The derelict and much damaged Barrington Court near Ilminster, described in 1904 as 'a shell, a wreck, and even in some places its oaken flooring has been removed' (together with its 'principal staircase'), was the first house to have been bought by the National Trust in 1907. It was given a full interior treatment by its first tenant, Col. Arthur Lyle from 1920 and this amalgam of elements from around England and Europe received unstinting praise in *Country Life* in 1928. Anderson Manor (1622) was being scrupulously restored from 1912. Cothay Manor, near Wellington, was 'brought back' at exactly the same time. What is unusual in Mapperton's case is that its restoration was the work of Henry Compton the ancestral owner, and not of a new purchaser.

The World War put a stop to any further plans that Henry Compton may have had for his Dorset estate. Melplash Court, with 1,118 acres appeared on the market within four months of the Armistice. Mapperton followed it in the summer, with a sale of separate farms on the estate in June and the house in August. In 1921 he was selling outlying cottages and small farms on the Minstead estate as well. The Mapperton estate was divided into eight lots, and each of the farms went their separate way with only Marsh Farm being bought by its tenant. The house, the advowson and two lots of 'good level

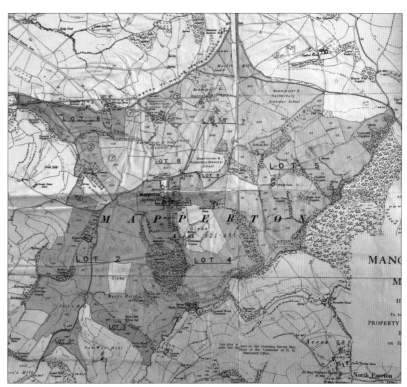

Map from Mapperton Sale Catalogue, 1919. [Dorset History Centre]

land' were bought by Mrs. Ethel Labouchère (1860-1955). She was the fifty-nine year old widow of Charles Henry Labouchère, a partner in Baring's Bank who, born in Holland, had died there during the war. They had been married for twenty years, but had no children. She was also the eldest daughter of a Scottish baronet, and sister of the mountaineer Sir Hugh Munro (1856-1919) who produced the first list of mountains over 3000 feet in Scotland, ever afterwards known as Munros. But she was fully familiar with Dorset for her parents had been living for twenty years at Fairfield House on the hill descending into Lyme Regis where her father had served as a JP; indeed the 1891 census catches Ethel at Fairfield with four other sisters and a couple of brothers, including the mountaineer. The sisters remained in the area and a memory is recorded of the four of them 'with their ear trumpets' at Mapperton in the 1950s.

The advertisement for the sale of Mapperton in *The Times* of 31 May 1919 had offered a selection of details likely to appeal to potential buyers. There was reference to 'ceilings emblazoned with armorial bearings' and 'oak panelled walls', not to mention two bathrooms. The stables were said to be 'singularly beautiful', and there were 'very comfortable' houses for Gardener, Keeper and Coachman. Outside, this 'Lovely Specimen of the Tudor and Jacobean Periods harmoniously blended' was surrounded by what were termed 'Inexpensive Gardens'. This ambiguous recommendation might spell relief to a potential purchaser whose interests lay elsewhere; to Ethel Labouchère it was perhaps a stimulus.

Gardens

The gardens at Mapperton are the creation of Mrs. Labouchère and Victor Montagu. Before 1919 references to gardens are scarce. 'Three gardens and two orchards' are mentioned in a marriage settlement of 1635 and Richard IV seems to have created parterres outside his newly classical north windows in the 1760s; their bones have been visible in years of drought. Richard IV was also responsible for the planting of a short-lived avenue stretching west from the house, visible on Isaac Taylor's map of 1765. Without owner-occupiers after 1775 it is

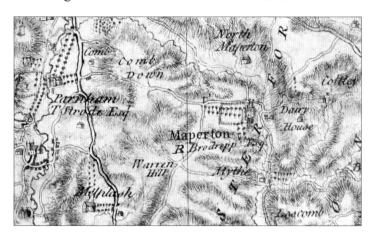

I. Taylor, map of Dorset 1765 – detail.
[Dorset History Centre]

not surprising that little was done to either house or grounds. By 1886 however a large glass house had been erected at the north end of the sunken valley that was later to be the site of Mrs. Labouchère's new garden. This was probably erected for Revd. Paulet Compton, who by then had occupied the big house for some years. The earliest photographs of the area, taken towards the end of Compton's life and perhaps in connection with the visit of *Country Life* in 1901, show a series of straight paths between rich flowerbeds along the bottom of the valley, while either side of the two long ponds below the retaining wall are given over to cold frames, vegetables and apple trees.

Mrs. Labouchère's principal focus of attention was to be the sunken valley that became the Fountain Court, but she also erected a summerhouse in the north eastern corner of the north garden, now called the Croquet Lawn, where the principal path down to the valley garden had always begun and the element of surprise, so like that associated since the eighteenth century with the Ha Ha, was at its most intense. The present yew hedge replaces an earlier beech hedge along the edge of the slope that renders the surprise the more complete.

Mapperton Gardens, view from north east, without hedge.

With a base at Lyme Regis Mrs. Labouchère was able to take her time to adjust to her new property and develop ideas about the garden. There were changes of personnel as ideas developed, but she appears to have been assisted by the young Dorchester architect Charles William Pike, who was working for Major Gundry on alterations at The Hyde, Bridport, in 1923. There's no other evidence in what is known of Pike's career up to the 1950s that he was interested in garden design, so that perhaps it was his surveying skills and draughtsmanship that Mrs. Labouchère intended to employ. Any drawings he did make are said to have been destroyed. The workforce she employed for the garden was recognised on a plaque placed close to the central pool. Names such as that of 'G. Gale, mason', could easily be connected with the

Mapperton Gardens, plaque commemorating builders, c 1927

Gale family of Loscombe who had been referred to as masons in each of the preceding three centuries, and Trevetts had featured often in the manor court in the late sixteenth century. The design, which seems to bear the influence of Harold Peto, was completed by 1927, the date on the dedication plaque to Mrs Labouchère's late husband and of a formal opening 'attended by smart London architects'.

Mapperton Gardens, central pool.

The area within which Mrs Labouchère's garden lay was defined to the north by the glasshouse, to the south by an existing retaining wall above the pools, to the west by the steep grass slopes and to the east by a wall of brick. Within that rectangle she placed a central octagonal pool, flanked by four stone acanthus and ornamental brickwork leading up steps to a pergola in front of the glasshouse and down to another pergola matching symmetrical one. The pool has a modest fountain, framed by four smaller Italianate fountains that help to frame it. Dominant now are the solid blocks of mature topiary, enlarging the central area,

Mapperton Gardens, topiary.

marking the flights of steps and achieving by combining box and yew an effective contrast of texture. A photograph of the 1930s shows that the grottoes in the east wall and the west slopes were later additions, in which chimney pieces were constructed re-using the arched heads left from the restoration of the windows of the main house in the 1900s. The garden was open to the public from at least 1930, when the *Western Gazette* claimed that Queen Elizabeth had bathed in a 'Roman tank' in the garden on her visit to Mapperton.

Below the retaining wall lay the two narrow rectangular pools, shown on the Tithe Apportionment map (1840) and possibly much older. Semi-circular yew hedges surrounding a rather small font-like centrepiece and statues of cranes were installed while the sides of the valley at this point were planted with fruit trees and vegetables. As Mrs Labouchère grew older and

Mapperton Gardens, rectangular pools, C18th, or earlier.

with the shortages of the second World War and the years afterwards the maintenance of this part of the garden declined.

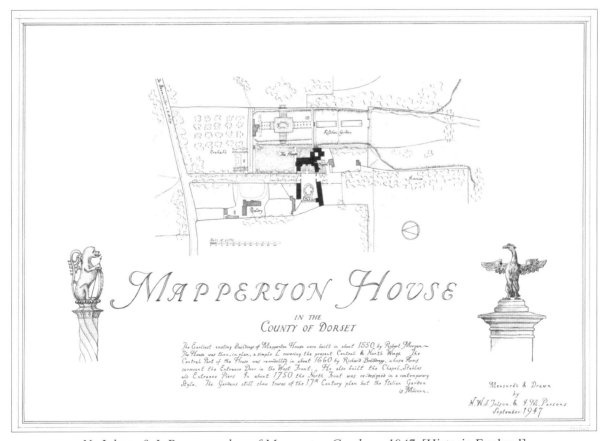

N. Jolson & I. Parsons, plan of Mapperton Gardens, 1947. [Historic England]

To the Present

When Mrs Labouchère died in 1955 the estate of 678 acres was sold by her nephew and executor, Lt. Col. N.E.P Sutton. It was bought by Viscount Hinchingbrooke (1906-1995), son of the 9th Earl of Sandwich, but better known as 'Hinch', or as Victor Montagu after he disclaimed his peerages on succeeding his father in 1962. Two principal considerations impelled him to Mapperton. His ancestral home, Hinchingbrooke near Huntingdon, was far too big and impractical for his needs and, as MP for South Dorset since 1941, he needed a house closer to his constituency. The Montagu family also had deep links with the area because since the nineteenth century they had owned the extensive Hooke estate next door to Mapperton and Montagu's father had paid neighbourly visits to Mrs Labouchère from the cottage he had built at Copse Barn, Wytherston.

Over the next decades Victor Montagu threw much of his abundant energies, foiled in politics, into the restoration and development of the garden. By 1966 two significant alterations to the Fountain Court were completed. The Victorian glasshouse was replaced in 1968 by a smaller and more elegant orangery at the north end on the axis of the central pool, and the pergola that had stood between the glasshouse and the pool was relocated to the south end where the oak beams of the structure are now rivalled by the massive branches of the wisterias it supports. The pool garden was radically cleared and the way was open for further development of the west side of the valley. The eastern shrub garden became Daniell's Garden, named after a Major Vernon Daniell who designed it, while to the south and west lay an arboretum that half a century later approaches maturity, offering in its woodland diversity of scale and variety of form a contrast to the late Edwardian symmetries of the Fountain Court. Further down the valley 'Hinch' created an important arboretum and a Spring Garden beyond.

The impact of Victor Montagu on the estate at Mapperton extended more widely than the sunken garden. The elm avenue running south from the road towards the house was replanted with limes and in 1962 a beginning was made in developing the view west from the house, once the site of Richard Brodrepp's avenue of *c.* 1765, by digging a ha-ha and the placing of a terracotta urn above it. This vista became much more visible, if not more developed, when the old walnut tree in the centre of the courtyard had to be felled in the 1970s.

Montagu also transformed the interior of Mapperton by bringing from Hinchingbrooke the contents of his ancestral home. The most complete transformation was achieved in the the Drawing Room. Here the import of a late eighteenth century marble fireplace to replace

Victor Montagu beneath old walnut tree, Mapperton.

the white painted carved wooden example from Richard IV's reconstruction of the 1750s complements the series of grand Montagu portraits. The difference made, especially by the Montagu portraits may be seen in a slightly unfair comparison between a black and white photograph of the room as Mrs. Labouchère left it, partly packed up following her death, and a modern view of the same interior in colour.

Contrasting views of drawing room, 1956 and 2021.

Victor Montagu died in 1995. His son John Montagu, and his wife Caroline, took over the management of Mapperton from the mid 1980s, giving up much of their professional work in London to the daily task of maintaining the Dorset property and farmland. Caroline devoted time to management of the estate: farms, buildings, tenanted properties as well as seeking grants for farm buildings and land and restoring the architectural balance in the Fountain Court and extending the arboretum. Meanwhile John (who had succeeded to the title of 9th. earl of Sandwich) took on the public access to Mapperton by opening the house, arranging tours and receiving researchers consulting the family archive.

The end of Coltleigh as a working farm in 1990 may be taken as a point at which income from farming at Mapperton ceased to make a significant part of the income of the estate. From then on the income from letting farmhouses and cottages began to make a greater contribution than did the fields around them. Several cottages had to be modernised for this new clientèle, but occasionally a novel source of income, from filming, facilitated the transformation. As John Montagu had wryly noted in 1988, 'Down at Burcombe the BBC has no less than 50 people involved in a few days filming... which will make a splendid contribution to rewiring that farmhouse.' More recently the big house itself has been used in the movies, most notably as Bathsheba Everdene's farm house in the latest remake of *Far From the Madding Crowd* when the entire stable courtyard and front garden were returned to a farmyard to achieve the desired effect.

Mapperton, forecourt as shown in From the Madding Crowd, 2015.

The management of the Mapperton estate has now been handed on to John and Caroline's son Luke Montagu and his wife Julie and they have brought not just their own talents but a generation's insights to its development. Almost at once they were confronted by the Covid pandemic which put paid to traditional ways of attracting visitors. Their response has been the creation of Mapperton Live, a website initially for subscribers, that produces a stream of short programmes about the house, its gardens, its heritage and its future. As an American, Julie brings infectious enthusiasm to explaining aspects of the estate which might otherwise be taken for granted. During lockdown this proved a brilliant means of making many aspects of the place (virtually) accessible to a wide audience.

Of all the plans for the estate that Luke and Julie are developing, including the modernisation of attic bedrooms to provide accommodation for yoga retreats, for any historical account such as this the most interesting concerns their plans for Coltleigh. Now an area of 180 acres, this farm has been hardly touched for forty years. Its hedges have grown wide, the land has not been ruthlessly drained, the mixture of ancient woodland and irregular fields is much as it has been for centuries. This area they propose to 'rewild' following the example of the Knepp estate in West Sussex which has developed this approach since 2001. The aim is to combat the loss of biodiversity, rather than to promote food production, and to regenerate the soil. White Park cattle have been introduced to graze but also browse on shrubs and trees, while Tamworth-wild boar cross will rootle in the soil to assist the regeneration process, and encourage insect life that will bring a host of other species in to feed upon them. This is all completely contrary to the way in which Coltleigh has been used for many centuries, but the experience of the last hundred years has shown that the land is quite unsuitable for the demands of 'agribusiness', while in a wider perspective informed by awareness of global warming and our loss of biodiversity this land becomes a means, in a small way, to help turn the tide. And this rewilded countryside can be marketed. Whether by 'glamping', wildlife safaris, or expert-led walks in search of rare orchids, the perennial or reintroduced specialities of this uncommon countryside will attract another generation of visitors alongside the traditional audience for a stately home, a unique garden, and tea.

BIBLIOGRAPHY

MANUSCRIPTS

The National Archives
C 6385/67 G. Brodrepp *v.* R Brodrepp et al.
MAF 32/467/30 Farm Survey: Mapperton, 1941
MAF 32/467/31 Farm Survey: Beaminster, 1941
PROB 4/11322 Inventory of John Morgan 1683
WARD 7/20/192 I.P.M John Morgan 1580
Wills.
PROB 11/49/271 Robert Morgan 1567
PROB 11/73/487 John Brett 1588
PROB 11/75/202 William Stourton 1590
PROB 11/77/172 Christopher Morgan 1591
PROB 11/88/38 Mary Stourton 1596
PROB 11/136/475 John Luttrell 1620
PROB 11/149/271 Richard Rose 1620
PROB 11/273/486 Richard Brodrepp I, 1658
PROB 11/305/76 Catherine Bradrepp 1661
PROB 11/395/461 Frances Tucker 1689
PROB 11/400/111 John Bradrepp 1690
PROB 11/491/386 Mary Brodrepp 1706
PROB 11/493/479 Richard Brodrepp II 1706
PROB 11/524/153 Robert Brodrepp 1710
PROB 11/615/136 Hugh Strode 1727
PROB 11/687/135 Richard Brodrepp III 1737
PROB 11/695/289 Henry Halsey 1737
PROB 11/829/329 Thomas Brodrepp 1757
PROB 11/1000/229 Richard Brodrepp IV 1774
PROB 11/1049/371 Mary Bradrepp 1779
PROB 11/1405/97 Revd John Richards 1804
PROB 11/1441/23 Bennett Combe 1806

Dorset History Centre
DC-BTB/F/5 Mapperton Court Roll 1638 -41
DC-BTB/F/6 Presentments to Mapperton Court
  1638-9
DC-BTB/F/7 Copies of Court Roll 1614-39
DC-BTB/F/8 letter of R Brodrepp I, 1640
MAP/M1/1 scrap of Account Bk. of R Brodrepp IV
MAP/CW/1/1 Mapperton Churchwarden's accounts,
  1774 ff.
D 1/9656 Marriage settlement of Richard Brodrepp,
  1608
D 1/9659 Marriage settlement of Bennett Combe 1735
D 1/9663 B. Pryce, map of Charity lands for use of
  Poor in Beaminster, 1776
D 1/9691 Marriage settlement of Christopher
  Brodrepp, 1635
D 1/9738 Will of R. Brodrepp, 1708

D 1/9822 Marriage settlement of Hester Brodrepp,
  1739
D-1061 J.B Russell Mss.
D-795/17 Sale Catalogue, Mapperton, 1919
D-697/1 Poll Book (copy) 1727

Hampshire Record Office
9M73/G340/20/1 letter from Earl of Shaftesbury to
  James Harris, June, 1765

Wiltshire and Swindon Archives
Dean of Salisbury Mss.
D5/28/7 Churchwardens' Presentments:
late C16 -1695
D5/10/2/10 Rectory Terrier 1628
P5/3Reg/17b 1573, will of John Mundeyn th'elder
P5/1594/63 will & inventory of Oliver Mundin
P5/6 Reg/68A 1594 will of John Mundin
P5/6 Reg/68B 1594 inventory of John Mundin
P5/1603/45 inventory of Roger Knight
P5/1619/85 will & inventory of Oliver Trivett
P5/1625/21 will of William Cake
P5/10 Reg 268A inventory of William Cake
P5/11 Reg/6C will of Hugh Munden
P5/1627/34 inventory of Hugh Munden1627
P5/13Reg/256C will of George Bowden
P5/1640/1 inventory of George Bowden
P5/1698/5 will & inventory of Bernard Banger

Mapperton House Ms.
Dick Berry's Memories of Marsh Farm, 1941-52

PRINTED BOOKS

A distinct and faithful accompt of all the receipts ... of the moneys collected ... for the poor distressed Protestants in the valleys of Piemont ... 1658

Calamy, E. *A Continuation of the Account of the Ministers .. Ejected and Silenced* 1727

Dod, P. MD. *Several Cases in Physick. And one case in particular giving an Account of a Person who was inoculated for Small Pox ... and yet had it again.* 1746

Hutchins, J. *History and Antiquities of Dorset.* 1774, 2 vols.

Young, A. *A Farmer's Tour through Eastern England ...* 1771 4 vols. III & IV

Risdon, T. *The Chorographical Description or Survey of the County of Devon.* 1811

Marshall, G. *The Rural Economy of the West of England,* 1796. II

Stevenson, W. *General View of the Agriculture of the County of Dorset, with Observations on the Means of its Improvement Drawn up for the Consideration of the Board of Agriculture.* 1812

Hutchins, J. ed. W. Ship & J. Whitworth, *History and Antiquities of Dorset,* 1861-1870. 4. vols. [Vol.II, containing Mapperton bears a title page dated 1863]

Maskell, W. *The Desecrated Chancel,* 1864

Gildea, Canon W. 'Mapperton', *PDNHAS* 1899 XX

Mayo, C.H. *The Minute Books of the Dorset Standing Committee, 23 Sept., 1646 to 8 May, 1650.* Exeter 1902

Pollen, J.H. Unpublished Documents relating to the English Martyrs Vol. I, 1584-1603. *Catholic Record Society* 1908

Lyte, H C Maxwell, *A History of Dunster* 1909

Hine, R. *History of Beaminster,* Taunton, 1914

Hodson, N. The Murder of Nicholas Turberville. Two Elizabethan Ballads. *Modern Language Review* 33 1938, pp. 520–27

Meekings, C. *Dorset Hearth Tax Assessments, 1662-1664.* Dorchester. 1951

Royal Commission on Historical Monuments. An inventory of the historical monuments in the County of Dorset I *West.* 1952

Lafond, J. Traffic in Stained Glass from abroad in the Eighteenth and Nineteenth Century. *Journal of the British Society of Master Glass Painters* XIV, 1964, pp. 58-87

Lloyd, R. *Dorset Elizabethans at home and abroad.* 1967

Short, B. *A Respectable Society, Bridport 1593-1835.* Moonraker Press, Bradford on Avon. 1976

Stoate, T.L. *Dorset Tudor Subsidies, Granted in 1523,1543,1593.* Dorset Record Society. 1982

Machin, R. *The Building Accounts of Mapperton Rectory.* Dorset Record Society. 1983

Clifton, R. *The Last Popular Rebellion; The Western Rising of 1686.* 1984

Manco, J. and Kelly, F. 'Lulworth Castle from 1700'. *Architectural History* 34, 1991, pp.145-170

Duffy, E. *The Stripping of the Altars, Traditional Religion in England, 1400-1580.* New Haven and London. 1992

Greaves, R. *Secrets of the Kingdom. British Radicals from the Popish Plot to the Revolution of 1688–1689.* Stanford, Ca. 1992

Kent, T.A. *West Country Silver Spoons and their Makers, 1550-1750.* 1992

Cole, W. Catalogue of North European Roundels. *Corpus Vitrearum Medii Aevii: Great Britain* 1993

Walsham, A. *Church Papists. Catholicism, Conformity and Confessional Polemic in Early Modern England.* Royal Historical Society. 1993

Penoyre, J. & J. *Decorative Plasterwork in the Houses of Somerset 1500-1700,* Taunton 1993

Roscoe, I. Peter Scheemakers. *Walpole Society* 61, 1999, pp.163-304

Vickery, A. *The Gentleman's Daughter. Women's Lives in Georgian England.* 1999

Dalton, C. *The Bells and Belfries of Dorset,* Part II, Upper Court Press, Ullingswick, 2001

Baird, R. *Mistress of the House, Great Ladies and Grand Houses.* 2003

Faraday, M. *Worcestershire Taxes in the 1520s: the military survey and forced loans of 1522-3 and the Lay Subsidy of 1524-7,* 2003

Diack Johnstone, H. 'Handel at Oxford in 1733' *Early Music,* 2003, pp. 249-261

Stephens, F. *Florrio.* Privately printed. 2005

Craske, M. *The Silent Rhetoric of the Body. A History of monumental Sculpture and commemorative Art in England, 1720-1770.* New Haven and London. 2007

French, H. *The Middle Sort of People in Provincial England, 1600-1750.* Oxford. 2007

Mills, A.D. *The Place Names of Dorset* IV [West Dorset]. 2006

Harris, J. *Moving Rooms.* New Haven and London. 2007

Stoate, T.L. *The Dorset Muster of 1569.* B. D. Welchman, Paignton, 2007

Yarker, G. *Georgian Faces, Portrait of a County.* Dorset County Museum 2010

Wood, A. *The Memory of the People. Custom and Popular Senses of the Past in Early Modern England.* Cambridge 2013

Hill, M. *West Dorset Country Houses.* Spire Books, Reading. 2104

Hill, M. Newman, J, Pevsner, N. The Buildings of England. *Dorset.* 2018

Montagu, J. *Mapperton Moments.* 2019

Goodall, J. 'The Lure of History' *Country Life,* 26 May, 2021, 80

ABBREVIATION

PDNHAS – Proceedings of the Dorset Natural History and Archaeological Society

INDEX

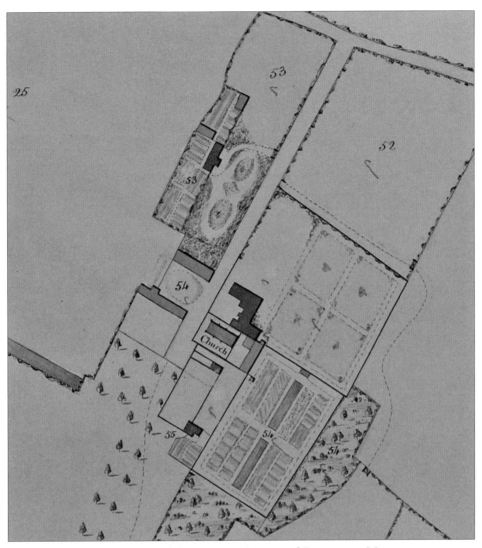

*The surroundings of the Manor House and Rectory at Mapperton,
as shown, slightly inaccurately on the Tithe Map of 1840.* [Dorset History Centre]